The Witches' Almanac

Spring 2016 — Spring 2017

CONTAINING pictorial and explicit delineations of the
magical phases of the Moon together with information about astrological
portents of the year to come and various aspects of occult knowledge
enabling all who read to improve their lives in the old manner.

The Witches' Almanac, Ltd.

Publishers   Providence, Rhode Island
www.TheWitchesAlmanac.com

Address all inquiries and information to
THE WITCHES' ALMANAC, LTD.
P.O. Box 1292
Newport, RI   02840-9998

10-ISBN: 188109832X
13-ISBN: 978-1-881098-32-4

ISSN: 1522-3184

First Printing July 2015

Printed in USA

Printed on recycled paper

Established 1971 by Elizabeth Pepper

Preface

IN THE PRESENT DAY, many are focusing on the next world crisis – global warming, financial catastrophe, drought, war, earthquakes, civil inequality and many other unpredictable and frightening matters. Differences in culture, location, race and gender are among the things that influence us when we direct our focus toward such things. Nevertheless, everyone is concerned with what the whole world thinks of the troubles around us – in a global community sense.

There is a division here, not just a division of the have and have-nots in a financial sense but a greater one; a division between the wise and the great pool of the unaware. The wise know how to balance their inner selves, where the unwise have no idea of such subtleties. As witches and magicians, we are aware that manifestation comes from the beyond into our mundane world, not the other way around.

Our attention should not only be on external issues — although that is a necessary part of living in the mundane world — but it should also be focused on the realm of the inner worlds. Peace does not come from without and influence the world within. It works in reverse. The peace found within grows to affect the world without. This is the way true world harmony will prevail. We must use our skills and talents in the astral and beyond to affect the conventional world. As either a force of Light, an individual in harmony with Nature, or the member of a secret society, we should all strive to bring peace, harmony and compassion to the world. Let us use all of our skills to reach this goal. Let us raise the consciousness of all people.

⌒ HOLIDAYS ⌒

Spring 2016 to Spring 2017

March 20 . . . . Vernal Equinox
April 1 . . . . All Fools' Day
April 30 . . . . Walpurgis Night
May 1 . . . . Beltane
May 8 . . . . White Lotus Day
May 9, 11, 13 . . . . Lemuria
May 20 . . . . Vesak Day
May 29 . . . . Oak Apple Day
June 5 . . . . Night of the Watchers
June 21 . . . . Summer Solstice
June 24 . . . . Midsummer
July 23 . . . . Ancient Egyptian New Year
July 31 . . . . Lughnassad Eve
August 1 . . . . Lammas
August 13 . . . . Diana's Day
August 17 . . . . Black Cat Appreciation Day
September 5 . . . . Ganesh Festival
September 22 . . . . Autumnal Equinox
October 31 . . . . Samhain Eve
November 1 . . . . Hallowmas
November 16 . . . . Hecate Night
November 17 . . . . Saturnalia
December 17 . . . . Fairy Queen Eve
December 21 . . . . Winter Solstice
January 9 . . . . Feast of Janus
February 1 . . . . Oimelc Eve
February 2 . . . . Candlemas
February 15 . . . . Lupercalia
March 1 . . . . Matronalia
March 19 . . . . Minerva's Day

Art Director . . . . Karen Marks

Astrologer . . . . Dikki-Jo Mullen

Climatologist . . . . Tom C. Lang

Cover Art and Design. . . . Kathryn Sky-Peck

Sales. . . . . Ellen Lynch

Shipping, Bookkeeping . . . . . D. Lamoureux

ANDREW THEITIC
Executive Editor

GREG ESPOSITO
Managing Editor

JEAN MARIE WALSH
Associate Editor

**JUDIKA ILLES,
ANTHONY TETH**
Copy Editors

⊂◯ CONTENTS ◯⊃

CONTENTS

Invocation to Diana

Diana, beautiful Diana!
Who art indeed as good as beautiful,
By all the worship I have given thee,
And all the joy of love which
    thou hast known,
I do implore thee aid me in my love!
What thou wilt 'tis true
Thou canst ever do:
And if the grace I seek thou'lt
    grant to me,
Then all, I pray, thy daughter Aradia,
And send her to the bedside of the girl,
And give that girl the likeness
    of a dog,
And make her then come to me
    in my room,

But when she once has
    entered it, I pray
That she may reassume
    her human form,
As beautiful as e'er she was before,
And may I then make love to her until
Our souls with joy are fully satisfied.
Then by the aid of the great
    Fairy Queen
And of her daughter, fair Aradia,
May she be turned into a dog again,
And then to human form as
    once before!

– Aradia: Gospel of the Witches
Charles Godfrey Leland, 1899

Aradia: Gospel of the Witches may be read in its entirety in *The Witches' Almanac* edition featuring an introduction by Professor Robert Mathiesen and new essays by notable modern Craft authors including Paul Huson, Raven Grimassi, Judika Illes and Dr. Leo Louis Martello.

Yesterday, Today and Tomorrow

by Timi Chasen

THE DARK SIDE. Do you believe your own eyes? Can you truly trust what you see? Even those well versed in the concept of hidden realities may still take for granted the solidity of the chair on which they sit, but the material world constitutes a mere sliver of the complete universe. Magic has long asserted the existence of planes beyond the material, and advances in science serve to confirm that intuition. Take for instance dark matter, which comprises over eighty percent of the known universe and yet cannot be observed directly. Dark matter neither emits nor absorbs light; its presence is known only through inference, when its gravitational force distorts the visible light of the cosmos. Several new dark matter mapping projects are currently underway across the globe, from teams and observatories as far flung as Chile, Hawaii, Japan, and the Netherlands. These mapping endeavors strive to create an accurate understanding of how dark matter is distributed throughout the universe. This information could lead to further revelations, such as the true nature of dark energy. If the existence of dark matter is only inferred, dark energy currently exists merely as speculation. Confirmation of the presence of dark energy could completely reshape our understanding of the nature of the universe. Until then, keep your eyes peeled for invisible forces.

ONE FISH, TWO FISH, COLD FISH, NEW FISH! It's common knowledge that the cold-hearted are at a romantic disadvantage, but did you know they were at a predatory disadvantage as well? The denizens of the deep sea are notoriously lethargic due to the extreme

cold temperatures slowing everyone down. Even the predators tend to take passive approaches to the hunt. Not so for the opah, a newly discovered deep sea predatory fish which zips around its cold environment like predators of much warmer climates. The opah's unique energy level is credited to its novel circulatory system, where heat generated by its flapping fins is used to warm blood vessels in its gills. The blood is pumped throughout the opah's body, making it the first warm-blooded fish ever found. While not warm-blooded in the same sense that mammals and birds are, their ability to heat their entire body is unique among fish. The opah can remain at a temperature several degrees hotter than its environment, allowing it to move faster, providing a predatory advantage over its competitors. Just one more reason not to be so cold-hearted.

ANCIENT CHINESE SECRET. Researchers at Harvard University have been diligently attempting to unlock the secrets of blue evergreen hydrangea root, a substance long used in Chinese medicine with promising results. Blue evergreen hydrangea root has been used in China for thousands of years as a treatment for malaria and other ailments. Researchers have identified and isolated the active chemical, halofuginone, which they believe is responsible for the blue hydrangea's healing properties. Halofuginone can block rogue T-cells from interfering with healthy cells and causing inflammation. Researchers hope that with new investment from a major pharmaceutical company, their discoveries can lead to effective treatments for a range of inflammatory diseases, particularly fibrotic diseases. Ancient wisdom is once again validated by modern science.

LIVED ONCE, BURIED TWICE. The fear of being buried alive may seem an unreasonable one in our age of modern medicine, where the proclamation of death is usually accompanied by the verification of machines and professionals alike. But in the not so distant past this fear was a well-founded one. Lacking the kind of advanced tools taken for granted today, doctors of the past would rely on their own senses of hearing (listening for a heartbeat), sight (observing the breath or lack thereof) and touch (feeling for a pulse). Of course, humans are fallible and mistakes were often made, so cautious loved ones would often hold vigil over the body for several days, just in

case. The truly deceased would eventually be verified through the sense of smell. Sometimes this vigil was not possible, as was the case for Margorie McCall. Doctors feared the illness that took her life would soon spread throughout the town, so Margorie was buried immediately. She was buried with such haste, in fact, that her wedding ring was left on her finger. Grave robbers arrived shortly after her funeral and attempted to cut the ring off her swollen finger, only to be startled when the corpse began to scream! The robbers dropped dead on the spot, leaving a bewildered Margorie to climb from her grave and find her way home. When she finally arrived her husband had much the same reaction as the robbers, dropping dead at the sight of his presumably deceased wife standing in the doorway. Margorie managed to live normally for many more years. Her gravestone bears the telling epitaph: "Here lies Margorie McCall. Lived Once, Buried Twice."

PRESERVATIONS. Though Margorie's ordeal was due to an honest medical mistake, some extreme ascetics of the past actually endeavored to be buried alive. The frightening act was the culmination of a years-long ritual referred to in the west as "self-mummification".

Practitioners were Buddhist monks striving to reach spiritual enlightenment. The ritual began with a one thousand day fast of seeds, fruits and nuts accompanied by strenuous physical activity designed to remove all traces of fat from their body. The next phase was an even stricter fast: one thousand days of eating only bark, roots, and resin. This diet promoted dehydration in preparation for the third and final phase, when the adherent, after entering a deep meditative state, is entombed in the lotus position and buried alive. After one thousand days, the tomb is unearthed and the body recovered. If

The Mummified Monk by Per Meistrup.

the body shows no signs of decay or corruption, it is taken as a sign of spiritual success and the body is revered; if the body has decomposed, then the spiritual goal was not accomplished and the body is reburied. The practice is most strongly associated with a particular sect of Shingon Buddhists in northern Japan, where successful adherents are revered as *sokushinbutsu*, or "living Buddha," but the practice has also been observed in Chinese and Indian meditative schools. Self-mummification is no longer considered an acceptable practice and is in fact illegal in Japan, though as many as six sokushinbutsu are still displayed – and revered – throughout Yamagata prefecture.

RESURRECTION. Earth is in the midst of a mass extinction. It is predicted that within the next century, half of all species on earth will disappear. The reasons for this mass extinction are myriad, but humans have had a definite role to play in its acceleration, particularly in the case of habitat destruction. Humanity's ever increasing need to house and feed a booming global population has led to the complete destruction of entire ecosystems, but efforts are underway to turn the tides. In New South Wales, Australia, The Threatened Species Reintroduction Project is striving to return native species to the outback. Under the new project, species that currently only exist as significant popu-

lations in captivity, such as the numbat, bilby, and brush-tailed bettong, will be reintroduced into protected areas in the hope that they can regain a foothold in their native habitats. The reintroduction of native creatures can do wonders to restore lost ecosystems. For example, the bilby and bettong, both burrowing mammals, will help the soil retain moisture and nutrients, thus helping vegetation in the area. Lost species have been reintroduced into landscapes before with promising results, such as when the gray wolf was reintroduced to Yellowstone national park. Only time will tell if Australia's efforts prove as successful. Here's wishing all you numbats the best of luck!

The Magic of Kohl

THE ANCIENT Egyptians expressed their love of beauty in their art and grave goods. The glow of the gold in Tutankhamun's death mask, off-set by vibrant blue stripes of lapis lazuli, has become an icon for the boy king, as well as the craftsmanship of the time. It's not only the precious metals and gems that one remembers, however, but also the dramatic eye makeup.

In ancient Egypt, the eyes of both men and women — and not just royalty — were lined top and bottom with a thick black powder known as *kohl*, *kajal*, or *mesdemet*. The outlined eye resembled the almond-shaped eye of the falcon god Horus observed in the Eye of Horus (*utchat*) glyph. This shape invokes the god's protection, warding off evil spirits and diseases of the eye.

Galena and antimony

Kohl was typically made from galena (lead sulfide), the most common of all lead minerals, and is still made this way in North Africa and the Middle East. Tables of magical correspondences list lead, which is associated with the planet Saturn, with protection and defensive magic. Talismans and protective seals of Saturn were documented in the *Key of Solomon*.

Antimony, possessing similar color and magical properties, is another mineral commonly used to make kohl in Egypt. As early as 3100 BCE, Egyptians were using antimony sulfide in eye cosmetics, so much so that the ancient words for antimony have kohl as their chief meaning. Other materials found in kohl could include aluminum, carbon, iron, zinc, camphor or menthol.

Illegal products

Though the ancients believed that kohl provided protection from evil and illness, high concentrations of lead in the finished product are quite dangerous. As recently as 2012, Boston Children's Hospital discovered a case of infant lead poisoning. Beginning when the baby was two weeks old, the parents had applied a Nigerian formulation to his eyes. Testing revealed that the preparation was 83% lead.

The US Food and Drug Administration bans kohl made from lead-containing ingredients; in other words, lead-based kohl is illegal in the United States. When you see an eye pencil labeled "kohl" on the shelf of your favorite cosmetic counter, the word refers to the shade or style of the pencil and does not mean that it is traditional kohl. Still, some illegal products do find their way to the shelves of shops specializing in imports, so check the label or ask the shopkeeper.

Soot and sandalwood

In India, kohl was made with soot rather than lead and contained ingredients believed to have medicinal properties in the Ayurveda and Siddha systems. This alternative preparation doesn't contain ingredients associated with Saturn, but was still considered effective against the Evil Eye and malevolent spirits.

One home recipe involved dipping an approximately four by four inch clean white muslin cloth in a sandalwood paste. The juice of *Alstonia scholaris* and *Manjal karsilanganni* are sometimes used instead of sandalwood.

Castor oil or ghee

The cloth is then dried in the shade, until sunset. At that time, a wick is made from the cloth and used to light a clay lamp filled with castor oil. A brass vessel is positioned over the flame, leaving enough room for air to circulate, so that the flame doesn't die out. This is left to burn overnight.

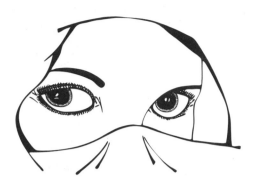

The next morning, one or two drops of castor oil or ghee (clarified butter) was added to the soot that had formed on the brass vessel. This mixture was stored in a clean, dry box.

What of the belief that the lead-based kohl of ancient Egypt was healthful? Surprisingly, when made properly with the correct proportions, it does have medicinal properties. Low doses of lead promotes the production of nitric oxide in the skin, which helps strengthen the immune system against eye diseases then common. However, as observed from the example of the 83% lead preparation used on the child in 2012, this can have the opposite effect when used in high doses.

Anti-glare stripes

The dark color of the kohl reduced the damage derived from sun glare, in much the same way that anti-glare stripes are thought to protect the eyes of American football players. (The jury's still out on that, however. Two relatively recent studies came to exact opposite conclusions.)

Do the modern no-lead concoctions have magical properties? Yes. Painting the eyes in the shape of the eyes of the falcon god still invokes his protection, and the color, likened to lead, still invokes the protection of Saturn.

– MORVEN WESTFIELD

Olokun

The mystery of the sea

THE YORUBA OF southwestern Nigeria have long honored a pantheon of deities (Orisa) that embody many natural features and phenomena. Among the plethora of Yoruba divinities, there is an enigmatic Orisa who transcends typical male/female polarity: Olokun, the divinity that inhabits the depths of the oceans and is the owner of all waters. This Orisa is a mystery embodying at times female energy, although at other times Olokun is clearly a male divinity. This association with both sexes is complicated not only by geography, but also by context of the mythology that surrounds it.

Trying to discover Olokun's identity by plumbing the root words that are the origins of its name is equally paradoxical. Olokun can be understood as a contraction of two Edo language words, *olo* meaning "owner" and *okun* meaning "the ocean," thus "the owner of the sea" which in this case is intrinsically male. Olokun could also be a contraction of *olio* meaning "queen" and *okun*, which, as we have seen, means "ocean" and thus literally "Queen of the Sea." Further complicating this latter translation is that she may be the consort, rather than regnant in this case. In Edo, the fact that most of the priests, other than the chief priests of the two main centers of worship are women tends to lend support to this view that Olokun is a female divinity.

Unfathomable wisdom

Perhaps the paradox that is Olokun's identity can be resolved by understanding that this mystery points to an intense knowing no individual can fully grasp the profundity of the sea and its contents. Knowledge of Olokun as a mystery is an understanding of unfathomable wisdom. That is to say, the instinct that there is something worth knowing that is beyond the parameters of humankind's simple categorization. Olokun's dominion of influence — like the sea that he/she rules — are those elements said to issue from the depths

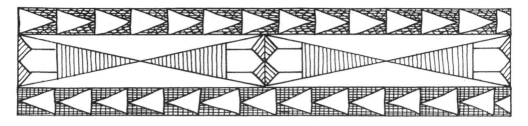

of its realm: wealth, psychic abilities, dreaming, healing and the very gift of life. Worshipped in Benin, Togo and by the Yoruba in Nigeria, his/her worship is amongst the most ancient. Olokun remains strong in modern day Lagos and the Olokun masquerades are among the main attractions at the Eyo festival performed there annually at a celebration known internationally.

In Edo Land, the women are attracted to Olokun mainly because this divinity is believed to grant children to them. This belief is so entrenched in Edo Land that, even today, most girls are not married until Olokun has been duly consulted and a proper worship performed. This, of course, is intended to ensure the marriage will be blessed with children. The bride, her parents and the groom consult the Orisa in a minor ceremony. In this blessing ceremony, Orisa are invoked upon the couple at the Olokun shrine of the bride's mother. If divination indicated that a major ceremony was necessary, the groom would then be required to provide money for the bride to be initiated into the Olokun cult so that she may have her own shrine.

Divinity of fortune

In all areas where Olokun is worshiped, this Orisa is seen as the provider of wealth. A common proverb states: "No one ever lives without knowing Olokun, except one who never spends money." Prior to the arrival of Europeans, the inhabitants of Yoruba Land, Benin and Togo used cowries as the means of exchange. This mollusk is found within the vastness of the sea, as well as within some rivers. It is no wonder that Olokun, the owner of the sea, is also the provider of wealth.

As well as being used for money, cowries are also used to indicate wealth by using them to decorate clothing. In fact, many priests of Orisa will decorate their clothing with cowries to indicate a spiritual wealth as well. It is clear that cowries, the symbol of wealth, come from the sea and other water sources, biologically furthering the property of the sea divinity. Olokun contains all wealth and is therefore the divinity of fortune.

It is said that Olokun is the wealthiest of the children of the creator god, Oludamare. In fact Olokun's wealth is only surpassed by Olodumare's. It is said

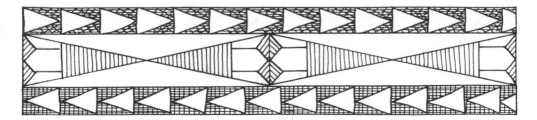

that at one point, Olokun believed "himself" wealthier than Olodumare. In Olokun's hubris, he challenged the Creator to a contest of wealth exhibition contest, which, invariably he lost, as related in this story:

The hosts of the sky had gathered to see who was wealthier. Olodumare then asked Olokun to list the items of his riches, which he did, thinking that his list would be longer than that of the Creator. After he finished compiling the list, it became the turn of the Creator to compile its own to enable the spectators to judge who was richer. First on the Creator's list was Olokun himself and all that it claimed as its own. Of course, the contest was given to the Creator without any difficulty for there was no point to contest with the one who owns you and all that you claim to possess. In consolation, Olodumare endowed Olokun with more wealth, power, wisdom and all that is needed to make life comfortable for humankind on earth.

This belief that Olokun is the source of wealth is so widespread that every wealthy individual is expected to worship Olokun. Traders, in particular, are expected to patronize Olokun. This is especially the case for those who make their money by means of the ocean. Many sailors will make offerings directly to the ocean, rather than to a shrine in their home.

It is also believed that general well-being comes from Olokun. Physical beauty and morality are also gifts of Olokun. Happiness and good luck are certainly considered blessings received from Olokun. White chalk which plays a prominent role in Yoruba culture is often given as a gift, expressing a wish for happiness, success and good luck. Is not uncommon for the Yoruba to grind up white chalk and rub it on their forehead as an expression of joy. Often when neighbors visit and see such a sign of joy, they too will rub some chalk on their foreheads to express complicity in the joy. In doing this, they are not only expressing empathy, but also a hope that Olokun will bless them as well. There is a prayer which expresses this:

Join me in rubbing on white chalk

*No danger in rubbing on white
chalk on behalf of one's friend*

*When you rub chalk, you do not
rub on charcoal*

*Charcoal is rubbed on,
on a day of mourning*

*But white chalk is rubbed on,
on the day of joy*

Olokun is also regarded as the divinity of morality and purity. Except for the red parrot feather that is worn on the forehead of an initiate, Olokun's priests wear only white as a sign of their purity. All of Olokun's priests are expected to be the embodiment of purity and honesty. It would be untoward for a priest of Olokun to wear dirty clothing. In fact, they are prohibited from eating until their body and their home are clean.

Just as the oceans are profound, so too, Olokun is understood as being the Orisa of profound wisdom. The following myth illustrates the depth of Olokun's wisdom:

Once upon a time, Olodumare (the Creator), sent Olokun to a river with a basket with which he was to fetch water home. Olokun immediately sensed the motive of his Creator and decided upon a plan to show he could not be fooled. Before he left for the river he got a piece of white chalk and drew some beautiful patterns on the ground in front of the house. Having done that he called out to the Creator with a request to remove the patterns spread out on the ground should it rain before he returned from the river. The Creator, who was apparently busy in the house, automatically promised to do so without knowing the type of patterns to which Olokun was referring.

Olokun set out for the river with a basket with which he was expected to bring back water. On getting to the river he took his bath and knowing the porous basket could not retain water, he started back for home with an empty basket. In the meantime, he caused rain to fall. The Creator, hearing that it was raining, hurried out to remove the patterns from the ground. Getting out, Olodumare discovered that they could not be removed and had undertaken to do so without ascertaining what they were. Olokun walked in with an empty basket soon after the rain and was asked why he did not bring water home. He asked the Creator why the promise was broken to remove the patterns in the event of rain. Olodumare confessed that it was not possible to do so. In the same way, said Olokun, it was not possible to fetch water with a porous basket.

Like the other Orisa, Olokun was carried to the Americas by the enslaved Yorubas, but held a special place in their hearts, being seen as their guardian during the Middle Passage, as well as the receiver of the dead for those who did not survive the arduous trip.

In the Diaspora, the stories evolved and Olokun took more attributes, becoming associated with the riverine Orisa, Yemaya. The following is a popular story of the association of Yemaya and Olokun association in the Diaspora:

In the beginning, there was only Olodumare and Olokun. Olokun was the progenitor of Yemaya. For a long time, Olodumare and Olokun fought for dominion of Earth. Whenever Olodumare sent something to the Earth, Olokun took control of it. Olodumare had dominion over all, however Olokun wanted to demonstrate that he/she had power over Olodumare, and to demonstrate this power, caused the sea to rise above the dry land. In order to return the Earth to existence, it was necessary to cool down Olokun. So terrible and powerful is Olokun that Olodumare asked Obatala to help restrain Olokun by fabricating seven silver chains to put around Olokun's neck. From that time onward, Olokun resides at the bottom of the ocean, next to a great marine serpent that shows its head when there is a new moon. It is Yemaya, the gentler side of Olokun that we see in the oceans. Olokun is believed to remain anchored down at the bottom of the ocean with seven chains. Whenever Olokun is enraged, he/she causes great damage. It is through Obatala's prudence that he/she is moored to the bottom of the ocean, but lest they lose wealth, humankind should not forget to worship Olokun.

In Yoruba Land, Olokun's mysteries and priesthood are very much alive. While a vestigial memory of the Middle Passage has left its mark on Yoruba descendants in the Diaspora. Olokun is so feared amongst the Diaspora that they will not even initiate an individual to the mysteries of Olokun. It is believed that no one can contain the profundity of the depths of the ocean on their head.

All of the above being said, the Diaspora do maintain lovely traditions for Olokun and do bestow the shrine of this Orisa to bring prosperity and a strong spiritual foundation to adherents of the faith. This is one of the most beautiful of rites among diasporic Orisa worshippers. It consists of taking the recipient to the sea for a cleansing and the imparting of a shrine that the whole community sees as a blessing, partaking of it themselves.

The next time you walk by the ocean remember the power of the sea, the wealth of the sea, and those souls who lost their lives to the sea. A Yoruba proverb perfectly captures it:

The monarch who resides inside the deep in majestic splendor is the name of Olokun Seniade (wearer of the most ancient crown)

— IFADOYIN SANGOMUYIWA

Prayer to Olokun when making an offering at the sea:

The Monarch of the Sea that is greater than an earthly monarch

Ugbolu Atetewere

The Monarch that owns abundant money

Ordinary ground that eats a cow

The street that has no faults

The spacious street

The provider of livelihood

The merciful provider for the poor

The giver that does not make the receiver feel little

The morning dew that makes yam and cocoyam flourish

Please, come in to accept offering

Sacred Synchronicities and Carrying On

THE UNIVERSAL mind, personified by witches as the voices of the Lord and Lady, constantly offers guidance and presents opportunities. When these messages are recognized and heeded, miraculous and wonderful events can unfold. When ignored, the flow of life might take a downward turn. Valuable opportunities are lost, leading to emptiness and regret. How often have you later lamented not calling a friend or making a purchase when you knew it was right? This is called the concept of synchronicity. It's simply going with the flow and being observant. It's moving forward when events occur and a situation feels right. There is a special magic about synchronicities. Often they are interpreted as signs or omens from subtle forces at work in the world around us.

A wonderful example of this took place several years ago. A young lady in high school obtained her driver's license and purchased a used car. Needing a summer job to pay the car loan, she went to apply at a fast food restaurant. The car broke down; she missed the interview and had to call Dad to the rescue. The car was fine when he arrived. The girl tried again, planning to apply for work as a bank teller. Again the car stopped running and Dad was called to the rescue. Again, the car started without a problem. When this happened a third time, Dad, who is very interested in metaphysics, realized that each time the car stopped running, it was in the same place: in front of a local modeling agency. This time, he told the girl to go into the agency and ask about work there. Reluctantly, being shy, exceptionally tall and gangly, she did. The agency recognized her potential immediately. Within a few weeks, she became a successful model for local advertisements. This dream job paid far more than the other positions ever would have.

Keep calm

An example of how heeding synchronicity can have a ripple effect, impacting the lives of millions of people, involves the popular mantra, "Keep Calm and Carry On." This catchy saying originated as World War II escalated, nearly

KEEP CALM AND CARRY ON

eighty years ago. It was part of a series of three civilian advisory posters prepared by the British government.

When the danger of a German invasion faded, nearly all of the red and white posters printed with the phrase were destroyed. Two generations passed and they were all but forgotten. Then something synchronistic and magical occurred.

It was the year 2000. Stuart Manley, a dealer in antiquarian books, purchased a very dusty old box at an auction. Mr. Manley thought the box was nearly worthless and was so unpleasant to sort through that he nearly discarded it. At the very bottom of the decrepit box, he discovered something that his wife found delightful. It was a single copy of the original poster. Mary Manley, an American who had married the Scotsman, who owned the bookstore, had it framed for display at Barter Books, the family's shop, located in the English village of Alnwick. The "Keep Calm and Carry On" poster drew the attention of customers who wished to purchase it. Barter Books began to offer reproductions for sale. For about five years the saying gained in popularity on a regional level. Then fate intervened again.

It was the 2005 Christmas holiday shopping season. A writer for *The Guardian* newspaper listed the poster reproductions among her top five favorite gift picks. This brought national and eventually international exposure. The saying became iconic and has taken on a life of its own. Since 2010 countless parodies of the phrase, as well as the original version, have erupted in all corners of the world. The warmhearted and welcome message inspires comfort, as well as confidence and courage in meeting life's challenges. Stuart Manley often jokes that he plans to have it carved on his gravestone.

– ESTHER ELAINE

Sonics & the Magic of Sound

USING OUR VOICES for magic comes as naturally as saying good morning to those you encounter on your walk through your day. The chief difference being, while you may mean, "Good morning and I hope your day is a good one," it is rare that you give your vocalization little more than a passing thought. That being said, your "Good morning" is impacted with the magic of hope.

The use of voice as a vehicle for magic is intrinsic, however, in order to load our vocalization with energy to create change we must load it with intent. Before we tackle sound, let's looks at how we accomplish magic and sorcery. Most magical acts are accomplished via a combination of three means:

1) Motion = Actions, Gestures, Dance
2) Sound = Your Charged Voice
3) Emotion = Scalding Will

When you think about it, you actually don't need any magical accoutrements to accomplish magic. Sound by itself greatly affects an environment. When charged with will and vibrated in a specific manner it becomes the only necessary tool, and one that is readily available at all times. Each of us has the ability to cause an effect with the use of sound whether you are leading a ritual or spell working or simply chanting before a divination.

Before discussing the application "will" it is important to talk about the physicality of sound. It is almost redundant to say that sound is a result of us breathing air in and expelling it allowing the larynx to vibrate, thus forming sound. However, as we know in a magical life, we want to be aware of the whole with its individual pieces.

In order to understand sound, you might want to take a moment to experiment with the physical action of making sound. Repeat the following phrase three times: "The rain in Spain falls mainly on the plain," while placing the flat of your palm on:

1) the diaphragm
2) the throat
3) the lips
4) the nose

First in the process of magically charging sound is dealing with the physical vibration. Vocalization should come from the depths of the belly. The vibration should happen from the diaphragm and vibrate upward and outward. To understand this principal, here is a little exercise. Take a moment to intone "ah". This should be done in your normal speaking voice, without any emphasis on the vibratory quality. Observe what it feels like. Now try this again, only this time you should allow the "ah" to come from the belly and allow it vibrate in your belly, then your throat. Maybe try making it a more baritone sound, with a strong emphasis on the vibratory quality.

As you can see there is a great deal of difference between a sound that is vibrated as opposed to a sound that is simply spoken. When a note/sound is vibrated it almost becomes palpable. Sound is a vibration, subject to physical laws. As sound moves through the air, it causes a physical change in the environment. How does it feel in your body, how does it change your mood? I'm going to ask that you indulge me one more time; vibrate the "ah" sound again. The difference in this third intonation is you should now take note of the affect it has on your mood/feeling.

When you are working on spell casting, you will want to be vibrating the sounds you make, whether it be a simple invocation or a chant. So far we have talked about the vibration of sound as a physical reality. This is important because vibration will act as a conduit for magical will that you will add. It is through this application that you direct your thought/magic.

The physicality of sound, like all vibrations, is governed by natural laws. On the esoteric side (magic and psychic operations), we are not outside the bounds of these natural laws. We are still applying the same laws and principles that govern electricity, chemical reactions and other natural forces. We are using some of the same principles. By taking into account standard physical laws such as the "Law of Conservation of Energy," you can predict, create and/or control effects in the physical, psychic or spiritual aspects of the universe.

Before launching into the effects of sonics and the use of will to direct your magical use of sonics, it is important to realize this particular branch of magic is like any other action in magic. It reacts in a certain manner partially because of the way in which we charge it with our will. The same is true if you use another force to create magic such as a candle (i.e. light) to cause a change. Remember, these are mediums to carry our will.

Another fine example of the use of sonics to create magic is the "casting of a circle." Many of us create a sacred space in which to work our will. When casting the circle you are doing magic. Whether you use a simple chant or some sort of standardized invocation, your will must fill the air. The waves of sound convey your magic outward in forming the circle.

23

An understanding of the basic concepts of sonics will enhance your daily life, your religious practice and your magical endeavors. Again, how do we accomplish our magic and sorcery. As stated above we accomplish it through, motion (dance, hand gestures, use of a wand or athame to punctuate), sound (your charged voice or other sound producing objects such as bells) and emotion (your will to create change).

Sonics can enhance or diminish the effectiveness of your efforts in various areas of your mundane life as well as your magical life. For many of us, words (and sounds) and magic are inseparable. For example, the use of sonics is also present in the use of bells or singing bowls. I know that three knolls of the bell helps to clear the air of unnecessary vibrations and in the same instance acts as a signal to the spirits around us that magical actions are about to begin.

A skilled invocant (be they witch, magician or sorcerer) when working with various sounds is emitting meaningful sonic energies directed toward some act. If they are acting in a group, those hearing them physically are acting as receptive relays sending the message backwards through themselves along their inner linkage with the contact they are all trying to reach. Whether in a group or alone, when a magician invokes or makes use of any sort of sonics, the sound moves out into the ether acting like a tuning fork creating a vortex of like energy. It is important to remember this basic principle when dealing with sonics — sound, however generated, is an energy form that produces effects on both the material and the psycho-spiritual aspects of the universe!

Sound when motivated by will is one the most important tools of a witch.

Quality of Sounds

Sound can be imbued with qualities that will enhance the magical intent of the magician. A careful application of these qualities can change what kind of charge a sound will carry. Below is a basic outline the charges of sonics and of the elements:

Air: This is a high pitched sound. It doesn't carry very well over distances and produces little or no vibratory effects and require careful attention to notice. This is a subtle vibration.

Fire: This is a shrill and cutting sound. You would classify this as clear or bright sounds that carry well over distance or through other sounds. They produce a noticeable (and often disagreeable) vibratory effects on the nervous system of those within ear shot and will grab the attention.

Water: This is a soft mid-range pitch and will have a caressing or stroking feel to it. Using this type of sound produces a very noticeable vibratory effect. It will carry well over distances and is very audible.

Earth: This is a very solid or heavy, low pitched (this type of sound is sometimes subsonic) sound. These sounds produce a noticeable effect in the bones and other solids. They usually carry poorly over distance.

Using the above as moderators to the sounds you produce can be an effective means changing the magic of your use of sonics.

Using a Voice of Command

The voice that you use in magic (sorcery or other rituals) should never be the voice that you use in your everyday voice. You will want to speak with a voice of command in a ritual setting. What is meant by this? It means that you speak with intent and that you are aware of the vibration of the sound that you are creating. Your sound, like a good singer, comes from the belly and vibrates from the depths out of your being. Correct use of sound in a commanding manner will create change in your psyche and your body. It will also create a change in the physical environment surrounding you, which in turn, because of resonance, will affect all three systems. It is a loop of energy.

Keeping the above in mind, if you do not use your voice of command correctly and with true intent, the effect will be more on you than the environment you are trying to affect. A basic principle must be kept in mind with sonics, as with all magical operation. The greater you focus attention on the terminal end of your magic, the less energy you will be left with. That being said, intense focus on the terminal end of your workings will create a reflective bounce back of energy. This should be shielded against either by the creation of a magickal circle or other means of warding.

Another use of the voice of command is to create a counter against energy coming towards you. In this instance, one would use sonics to neutralize energy that is inbound. We often do this in a reflexive way in our everyday life. As example, when you find a close relation is doing an especially irritating action you might blurt out "cut it out." If done with force/authority, the effect very often is an immediate cessation of the action. You can use this very same forceful voice to counteract any magic which you feel coming your way by using a low pitched, highly charged burst of voice to shield yourself. I would caution that such a use should be infrequent and judicious as it can immediately stop anything in its path.

Let's go back for a minute to casting a circle or creating sacred space in which to work our magic. As stated earlier, we use sonics to cast the circle and once the circle is cast, it can act as an echo chamber increasing the vibratory affect. This is an effect many are aware of that use this method of magical work.

If you are calling the names of Gods or using words of power, they should be imbued with a vibrational quality that draws the energy that you are focusing on near. In the case of calling on various Gods, you will want to make your invocations like that of a primal scream issuing forth from the core of your being. A good way to experiment with this is say the name aloud without any want or desire and notice the effect. Try this again, imbuing your voice with a total want. Is there a change in the sonic quality of your voice? In the latter your voice should be shooting forth in a vibrational ray that catches the quality of the deity being invoked. Remember, focus and intention will necessarily change the sonic quality of your call. Two simple rules to keep always in mind:

1) The greater you focus on an intended recipient, the less energy you are left holding.
2) The greater your interest — focus on others' output, the greater the incoming energy load you receive and must handle (this is especially true of sorcery).

To make full use of sonics, I suggest the following three steps for the successful use of sound as method:

1) Take a deep, full breath and concentrate your consciousness in your heart.
2) Feel the word or chant in your very core (as if the letters are flaming red on your soul).
3) Emitting the breath slowly, pronounce the letter so the sound vibrates within, swelling into the space around you to fill it completely, radiating outward until it fills the universe itself.

Sonics can truly improve your magic in very predictable ways. To this end, in closing, you might want to take the time to go through your magical vocabulary humming words, chants, incantations and names to get yourself used to the use of vibrational techniques.

– Gwion Vran

26

Nyctophilia or the Love of Night

TRAFFIC NOISE dies down. Birds' song ceases and squirrels' chatter stills. The air becomes moist; you can feel it touching you. Night is falling and instead of mourning the dying day, you find yourself invigorated.

You may call yourself "night owl" or "child of the night," but there's another word for those drawn to the darkness, especially for those who feel sexual arousal when the black cloak of night descends: Nyctophiliac from the Greek *nycto*, meaning night, and *philos*, meaning fondness or attraction.

Is it surprising that many witches are nyctophiliacs? The notion that magic is more prevalent and magicians more powerful after the sun sets is an old and respected belief, so much so that the hour of midnight is called the Witching Hour.

Spirits are easier to communicate with after dusk, especially those who have gone before. Think of it: how many séances are conducted at high noon?

– MORVEN WESTFIELD

Herbs of Air

THE SUN RISES and triggers a soft breeze from the east. It carries to you the aspirations for the day. What will you accomplish? What is your aspiration? Where will it take you? A deep inhalation of soft whisperings of sage, lavender and mint, sparks your inner fire. Your exhalation releases power into the breeze. The breeze carries your intentions. Air conspires with you to create your world. Herbs and the other green growing ones can help you to attune your thoughts and willpower to manifest your desires. The herbs of air are our allies in our new beginnings, fueling ideas and thoughts, inspiring you to move forward in a new and determined manner.

Working with herbs starts with the mindful harvest. If you are harvesting from a wild source, be careful to only take less than one-third of a plant stand for your stores. Mindful is the key word. Be sure to ask if it is okay to harvest from the stand of herbs and listen with your open heart for the answer. Always return the favor, when harvesting from your plant allies. You can bring along a bottle of water and offer a cool drink on a hot day in thanks. Other offering suggestions include small crystals, coins, scoops of compost, a song and so forth.

Wavelengths of energy

Our relationship with plants is a symbiotic one. Without the oxygen they provide for us through photosynthesis, we could not survive. Keeping this in mind during harvest is the first step toward recognizing our deep connection to the plants and honoring them. It is important to give back during the gift of the harvest. No one wants to start their herb work by triggering resentment in the green ones!

Alignment of purpose to your working begins with setting your intention with the herbs that you will use. Speak to them. Sing and chant your desires. Get everyone and everything on the same page. It may seem silly to speak aloud to your herbs, especially after drying, but think of it as vibrations being carried through the air to settle on what will you be using; wavelengths of energy infusing your intentions into the plants matter.

Herbs in use

Putting your herbs of air into use can vary widely, depending on your needs and your surroundings. A popular route is to create a blend of herbs, based around their magical properties, infuse them with your intention, and burn them. This can be a wonderful and effective route, unless you set off fire alarms! Few things bring herb magic to a sudden end like the fire department or a concerned neighbor banging on your door.

How about a bath as another way to utilize your air friendly herbs? Create a blend of non-toxic herbs, wrap them in a muslin bag, or create a pouch from an old face cloth and secure with a hair elastic. Combining herbs of air with a warm soothing soak in water may be the ultimate relaxation bliss, quieting mind chatter and bringing a sense of peace and relaxation. All those stressful moments will be cleared away right down the drain! Who doesn't love the luxurious feel and scent of rose petals floating on the water?

New beginnings

Formulating oils and liquids using herbs that are aligned with air can be satisfying and effective. You can macerate a dry herbal blend in oil for anointing candles and mojo bags. These can be prepared in a slow cooker or double boiler. Alternatively, bring in the Sun's energy and warmth by setting a jar in the Sun. A "new beginning" oil, created at sunrise on the Spring Equinox, and set in the Sun for a few days would be wildly fueled with both herbal properties and the increasing Sun — a true force to be reckoned with!

In addition, an infusion in water or alcohol could be made the same way and is wonderful for use in spray bottles.

Cleansing and purification sprays work wonders in situations where a smoky white sage clearing of space is insufficient to remove negativity. The benefit of a water or alcohol infusion spray is immeasurable in its ability to be used in a hospital room, baby's room, offices, hotel rooms or any place where cleansing needs to go undetected by smoke alarms and smoke-sensitive people.

Mojo bags, amulets and poppets can all be stuffed with herbs of air. This technique is particularly useful for exams, to promote clear mental acuity, calmness and wisdom. You have the added benefit of being able to write out your intention and wrap your herbs in your writings, before placing them into your bag or charm. Aromatic herbs work best for this as you have a constant reminder of your charm as it triggers your olfactory nerves.

A few other suggestions for using herbs aligned with air:
• Scatter them across your floors and then sweep them up. This gives you a visual focus for clearing your space energetically and physically.
• A walking meditation on the beach or in a forest, charging your herbal blend as you go, and releasing it to the wind, is beautiful and symbolic, as the breeze carries your intentions to their fulfillment.

• A slow and steady release of power could be achieved by adhering herbs to a pillar candle and burning it over a period of time. This is a nice option for long term protection or healing, as well as a loving gift for a wedding.

Some common herbs of air:

Almond (*Amygdalus communis*): wealth, prosperity, money, material objects, love, fertility, aphrodisiac, compassion.

Anise seed (*Pimpinella anisum*): cleansing, youth, clairvoyance, consecration, divination, fertility, gain, good luck, money, nightmare prevention, protection, psychic protection and enhancement, aphrodisiac.

Benzoin (*Styrax benzoin*): cleansing, exorcism, prosperity, inspiration, spell-breaking, peace of mind, tranquility, psychic protection, wisdom, harmony, memory.

Black Haw (*Viburnum prunifolium*): weather magic, connecting with other planes of existence.

Caraway (*Carum carvi*): Sensuality, reviving passion, keeping love, protecting relationships, fertility, aphrodisiac, keeping secrets, protection from theft, honesty.

Catnip (*Nepeta cataria*): dreams, sleep, rest, peace, love, commanding, animals.

Elder Flower (*Sambucus canadensis*): magic, messages from the dead, psychic protection, clairvoyance, transformation.

Fennel (*Foeniculum vulgare*): confidence, courage, strength, longevity.

A perfect herbal ally to bring along for a job interview.

Gum Arabic (*Acacia senegal*): protection, psychic powers.

Henna (*Lawsonia inermis*): renewal, beauty, gentleness, gain.

Hops (*Hummulus lupulus*): sleep, visions, peace.

Horehound (*Marrubium vulgare*): healing, protection, mental powers.

Lavender (*Lavandula officinalis*): protection, peace of mind, love, virility, cleansing, consecration, relaxation and sleep, psychism, good luck, protection, divination, clairvoyance.

Lemon Verbena (*Aloysia triphylla*): happiness, lifting of spirits, joy, success, increases power, love, magic, dreams, nightmare prevention. The clear quartz amplifier of the herb magic world.

Linden (*Tilia spp.*): stimulates, lifts spirit, gladdens the heart, luck, strength, protection, sentinels, guardians.

Marjoram (*Origanum marjorana*): love, peace, psychic protection and development, happiness, protection, tranquility, weddings, brightens disposition, animals. Marjoram has strong associations with bees: if you need to be busy as a bee, this is your go-to herb!

Mint (*Mentha piperita*): restoring energy, lifting a heavy mood, relieving depression, renewal, release, good luck, happiness, connecting with animals, bringing money and prosperity, protection of belongings.

Mugwort (*Artemisia vulgaris*): magic to prevent theft, dreams, divination, clairvoyance.

Oak Moss (*Evernia prunastri*): luck, money.

Pennyroyal (*Hedeona pulegioides*): release and endings, peace and tranquility, restoring harmony.

Pine (*Pinus spp.*): honor, strength, honesty.

Primrose (*Primula officinalis*): stop gossip.

Red Sandalwood (*Pterocarpus santalinus*): meditation, revelation, cleansing and consecration, good luck and success, divination, connecting to other planes.

Rose (*Rosa spp.*): love, aphrodisiac, weddings, keeping secrets, peace, clairvoyance and psychic work, connecting with Ascended Masters. Roses come in many colors and scents; working with specific colors, scents and growth habits helps to fine tune your workings.

Sage (*Salvia officinalis*): immortality, wishes, longevity.

Savory (*Satureia hortensis*): use to attract males, fertility, gain love, increase passion and romance.

Star Anise (*Illicium anisatum*): luck, power, monetary gain.

Violet (*Viola odorata*): modesty, fidelity in love, honesty, sweetness, purity, rejuvenation, carefree attitude, releasing old patterns to return to a place of peace.

White Sage (*Salvia apiana*): cleanses, balances energies, purifies and protects.

Some recipes to enjoy:

Sweet Dreams Pillow Spray: Make an infusion of lavender, mugwort, lemon verbena and linden. Cool, strain and place in a spray bottle.

Money Bag: Gather oak moss, almond, star anise and mint and wrap them in a gold bag. You might throw a few coins in this one as well and keep it in your wallet!

Bag O' Brains: Print out a page from an article on the subject you are studying. Roll benzoin, lavender and fennel toward you and then tie it up. Bring this herbal pouch with you to exams, but don't forget to study!

– LILITH HEARTHSTONE

THE NINE ELEMENTS

Ancient Celtic symbols and spirits

MUCH OF OUR modern magical arte is grown from the symbolism of medieval and renaissance Europe, inherited from the very end of the Pagan age of Rome. In this we find the familiar pattern of twelve zodiacal signs, seven planets and, of course, four elements. This pattern has influenced occult symbolism from the early Middle Ages right into modern Pagan and witchcraft work today.

Those of us in the Pagan revival who look to a more ancient model have begun to work with triads of symbols. Rather than think of earth, water and air, we speak of land, sea and sky. Rather than find a fifth element for the center of a cross, we place the sacred fire in the center of the ancient triple spiral called the triskelion, meaning 'three-legged.' Land, sea and sky, with the fire in the sacred center — a more archaic approach to a core symbol in Pagan Europe.

To the ancients, the 'elements' of the world were the things from which all other things are made. Centuries of attempted science, healing and magic were built on these symbols. However they were never the only set of 'elements' in use. Again, a more archaic stratum of symbolism reveals a very ancient story as the basis for a more complex set of symbols.

Pagan lore preserves a motif that seems to reach back into the earliest strata of Indo-European cosmological thought – the idea that the cosmos, and, by reflection, the human self, is composed of the elements of the body of the first being, who is sacrificed or murdered in the creation of the cosmos. Across the Old World, we find lists of these elements, in which components of the natural world are corresponded with components of the human self. I have adopted a conventionalized list of nine components, or elements – *dúile* in Irish. I give the Irish for each, as well as the English:

Element	Irish	English
Stone	*cloch*	bone
Soil	*talam*	flesh
Vegetation	*fasra*	hair
Sea	*muir*	blood
Wind	*gaeth*	breath
Cloud	*nel*	brains (thoughts)
Moon	*eisce*	mind
Sun	*grian*	face
Stars	*rind*	spirit

It has long been customary to attempt to classify the spirits according to the divisions of the natural world. The most common of these in the occultism of the last 1000 years have been the seven planets and the four Classical elements; sylphs, gnomes, salamanders and undines are well-known even to modern occultists. In an effort to understand the spirits from a more broadly Pagan perspective and move back past the heavily Christianized magic of the renaissance magicians, we might consider using the *dúile* as a way of examining the spirits. Initial work suggests a good fit for the nature spirits of traditional folklore.

So in this short piece I will attempt to fit some of the well-known types of land-wights, or nature-spirits, or Sidhe-folk, into the Nine Elements of Druidic symbolism. In many cases this is a simple matter, and it sheds light on the nature of the spirits and how they fit into the cosmos. It also opens up some surprising vistas and reminds us why the third Kindred isn't just 'everybody else'.

The Nine *Dúile* are easily assigned to the Three Worlds:

The Land

Stone: Trolls, giants, mountain wights.

Wights of Stone are among the eldest and strongest beings. Mountain spirits are vast, if sleepy powers, who can shake off human effort like leaves from a dog's back. Lesser spirits of stone may still be trolls: unwholesome beings who like nothing better than to crack skulls. Some kinds of miners and delvers may also be of stone, but they may also be one of the following types:

Soil: Dwarves and goblins, spirits of fertility and rot.

Many of the kinds of spirits called bogles or goblins or various 'brown men' of the wood seem likely to correspond to the soil. They see to the power of growth for root and seed, but they also are consumers, eaters of corpses and clearers-away of messes. Most 'house bogies' and their ilk come from this type or perhaps from the next.

Vegetation: Dryads, green-jacks, corn-men and women, willow-devils and so forth.

Perhaps the most common of the land wights are vegetation spirits, present almost everywhere humans go. Folklore is full of flower-spirits and thorn-spirits and the spirit of the grain that is honored every year might be a 'god' in the conventional sense, but he or she is also the spirit of the grain itself, as a vegetation spirit.

The Sea

The Sea is full of spirits in the world of the insular Celts, from the selkies of the north to the merrows (mermaids and mermen), to various talking fish and enchanted beings. The sea is alien to mortals, and always dangerous and strange, although potentially a source of riches and a road of quests. Out on the wide sea the marvels of the weather, of nearby sky, become apparent, leading to the other two elements in this world.

Wind

The kinds of beings called trooping Sidhe, who riot through the air in their rade, carrying that which they pick up, are beings of the wind, as are messenger spirits, the winged ones who bear the word across the worlds. The Gaels

had detailed lore about the winds and we could focus on very specific spirits for the twelve winds, but even considering four classes of winged wind-beings for the Gaelic airts is interesting.

Clouds

What are cloud-spirits? They are bearers of weather, surely, often the great forces of the lower airs that carry the waters of the world across its face. More giants, perhaps, of the storm variety, grey and filled with lightning or low and daylight-quenching. Another system well outside the little reach of our senses, for the most part, although perhaps they hear us when we ask well.

The Sky

Moon — The moon is given to the cool, clear light of the quiet mind, uninflamed by the passions, still and shining. The spirits who dwell in the moonbeams are the night people, a part of what we might call the Noble Court or the High Sidhe. Along with the other sky beings, they carry the offerings and prayers of mortals to the gods, and bring back their blessings in turn.

Sun — The Shining Court are great but perhaps remote, walking bright and proud over the land, bringing warmth to soil, stirring wind and sea. These great powers, of Moon and Sun, may not be 'gods' per se, but the spirits, the daimones, of these elements are always present, always powerful beings in the order of the worlds. When we see them in later folklore, I believe they appear as 'angels,' and probably appeared as 'gods' to Pagan folks before that. Perhaps they do, in fact, do the business of the gods.

Stars — To speak of the nature spirits of the starry heavens is to open the whole question of the meaning of the seven planets and the many powerful fixed stars of European tradition. We have little indication of an important tradition of planetary symbolism among the Celts and Germans, yet it seems unlikely that the widely-learned Druids wouldn't have picked up the basics from the Greeks. In any case, besides those traditional bodies of lore, we can only contemplate what a spirit of the light of the stars on a summer night might be or do.

One immediate question in this arrangement might be "where are the animal spirits?" It seems to me that beasts are like us; they are beings of bone and blood and breath, none of which are shared by the vegetative form of life. So when we encounter animal spirits, perhaps they are in fact the 'ancestors' or 'the dead' of another species, choosing to help humans. Often I think they are guises worn by a god or spirit, often a spirit of soil or the green wearing the forms that live upon their power. Spirits of sun or moon may come as beasts to better address our human mind and personality. The ancients seem to have seen the spirits using animal forms – especially wondrous or monstrous hybrid forms – and in these cases the characteristic animals of the element become symbols of the spirits' power. It is entirely reasonable in traditional Pagan lore to envision such spirits as human forms with wings or horns or hooves or fishtails.

This classification system also offers us some approaches to practical magic and conjuring the spirits. When we design rites and spells we can refine our focus and call more directly to those beings and energies that can best aid our work.

A quick consideration of the possible practical magic associations of the *dúile* might produce:

Stone — works of permanence and protection. Difficult spirits, but strong. Be careful of your protections.

Soil — works of fertility or of decay. Good spirits for service and productivity, along with those of the green.

Vegetation — Works of sustenance, healing and vision. Important to maintain reciprocity with these spirits (as with all).

Sea — Not many practical works for land-dwellers among the strange beings of the Sea. Shore-dwellers and sailors will know more than I.

Wind — Works of communication and distant vision. Messengers and raiders.

Cloud – Weather-working in an immediate sense, but many clans of spirits are involved there.

Moon — Works of vision and mystery, initiation and meditation, secret rites and night-sacrifices.

Sun — Works of growth, strength and mastery, weather-work together with wind and cloud, spiritual perspective and memory.

Stars — Works of spiritual power. If one is willing to consider astrology, the whole realm of stellar and planetary powers might be present in this final, highest and strangest world.

In the process of developing a Celtic sorcery and spirit-arte, a central problem is classifying and identifying the spirits. In applying a wider set of categories than the usual four elements, we can more precisely locate the nature of the various beings told of in lore. With this beginning, we can better understand the nature of the kinds of spirits and we can more clearly honor them and know which of them to ask for aid in what ways.

– IAN CORRIGAN

The Akashic Records

Three Fates born from desire, weaving the Threads of Life from a spindle
But it is thou that carves one's own destiny with hammer and chisel
For the Moirai shalt cut the thread and end thou eyre

❧❧❧❧❧❧❧

THE AKASHIC RECORDS can be considered the magnum opus of the Divine. Why? Because not one single Supreme Being has dominion over them. Located within the astral plane and existing since the dawn of time, these archives can be accessed by clairvoyants and immortals. The Akashic Records contain every thought, action, intention and event in the history of existence. Etymologically, the term Akasha derives from a Sanskrit word meaning "Sky" or "Æther" but in Buddhism this term can also be defined as "space." Regardless of its meaning, the Akashic Records came to be known as a location where all memories and events in the history of the universe are rediscovered.

Edgar Cayce referred to the Akashic Records as the 'Book of Life' and utilized these records to unveil occluded mysteries of the past and make predictions of future events. Once a record was accessed, Cayce would use what portions were relative to the individual receiving a psychic reading. They can be perceived as hidden memories from past lives or as all dormant ones within the history of society.

Cayce says:

Upon time and space is written the thoughts, the deeds, the activities of an entity — as in relationships to its environs, its hereditary influence; as directed — or judgment drawn by or according to what the entity's ideal is. Hence, as it has been oft called, the record is God's book of remembrance; and each entity, each soul — as the activities of a single day of an entity in the material world — either makes same good or bad or indifferent, depending upon the entity's application of self towards that which is the ideal manner for the use of time, opportunity and the expression of that for which each soul enters a material manifestation. The interpretation then as drawn here is with the desire and hope that, in opening this for the entity, the experience may be one of helpfulness and hopefulness. (Reading 1650-1)

In his book, *Esoteric Buddhism* (1884), Alfred Percy Sinnet described the Akashic Records as "a permanency of records in the Akasha." Theosophists were deeply fascinated with them. Helena Petrovna Blavatsky suggested that they were tablets constructed from a sort of life force from the astral plane containing impressions and actions of the past and future. But maybe the most influential theosophical quote regarding the Akashic Records came from Alice A. Bailey, the one who most likely coined the term.

The Akashic Record is like an immense photographic film, registering all the desires and earth experiences of our planet. Those who perceive it will see pictured thereon: The life experiences of every human being since time began, the reactions to experience of the entire animal kingdom, the aggregation of the thought-forms of a karmic nature (based on desire) of every human unit throughout time. Herein lies the great deception of the records. Only a trained occultist can distinguish between actual experience and those astral pictures created by imagination and keen desire. (Light of the Soul — The Yoga Sutras of Patanjali: Book 3, Union achieved and its Results)

Akasha itself can be described as an essence and creative force existing in all matter, energy, thought, and spirit. All beings have Akasha, and in essence, it is the force that springs forth under the creative urges of the Divine Self.

Viewing the Akashic Records is similar to observing an event, as if one were actually present. A divine soul can travel to the permanent origination point of that which vanishes with time; that which time cannot be eradicated. They can broaden their perspective on reality and the understanding of history when one is not limited to merely the accounts of claimed witnesses and authoritative writers. At this point one can perceive events as they were but it takes a disciplined doyen to distinguish the difference between actuality and astral illusions. Through transitions from mortal thought to immortal experiences along the time line of all existence, history is scribed in many forms other than the mundane. Difficulty arises for one that only views the world materialistically and maintains a disbelief that a spiritual realm indeed exists. Those that can see through this will be able to understand all events in their pristine (immortal) form. History does not stand before her like meaningless events that no longer exist but appear as vivid experiences lasting eternally. In essence, what once was, takes place right before him within his dreams or thoughts.

Thoth is the deified historian in the stars that penned the Akashic Records. All emotions, experiences, thoughts, behaviors and events regarding past lives are contained within the records along the time line of the cosmos — Plato referred to this as *anamnesis*. Throughout history the Akashic Record has become a salient resource to a myriad of clairvoyants.

— Mario Salazar

The Cursed Amethyst
&
Other Cursed Gems

THE NATURAL HISTORY Museum in London enthralls visitors from its very entrance with a dinosaur skeleton replica and the astounding architecture of Hintze Hall. Cathedral-like in structure and height, it dwarfs the collection it houses.

If you are lucky enough to visit this grand institution, pause to take it all in, but when your neck is sore from craning to see the stories-high skeleton, continue to the grand staircase in front of you. Savor the walk up marble steps, being mindful that millions of visitors over more than 100 years have trod these same steps. At the top, take a right to the Green Zone and look for the Vault gallery.

Heron-Allen's cursed amethyst
The Vault gallery's collection of diamonds and gems, crystals, metals and meteorites from all around the world includes what is sometimes called the Delhi Purple Sapphire. The Museum calls it Heron-Allen's cursed amethyst, giving us, in reverse order, the actual nature of the stone, the reason for its notoriety, and the name of the last owner.

Edward Heron-Allen, a scientist and friend of

Oscar Wilde, obtained the gem from Colonel W. Ferris of the Bengal Cavalry. Ferris received it after it had been looted from the treasure of the temple of Indra at Cawnpore during the Indian mutiny in either 1855 or 1857. From the moment he acquired it, his life took a downturn; he lost both his money and his health.

Heydon's magic Tau and ring
His son fared no better, suffering persistent hard luck after inheriting it. He gave it away to a friend who then committed suicide. At that point, the son persuaded Heron-Allen to take it. He did, but unlike the others, he knew a bit about magic and curses and took precautions. The stream of bad luck stopped, but not all was quiet:

"From the moment I had it, misfortunes attacked me until I had it bound round with a double headed snake that had been a finger ring of Heydon the Astrologer, looped up with Zodiacal plaques and neutralized between Heydon's magic Tau and two amethyst scaraboei of Queen Hatasu's period, brought from Der el-Bahari (Thebes). It remained thus quietly until 1902, though not only I, but my wife, Professor Ross,

W. H. Rider and Mrs. Hadden, frequently saw in my library the Hindu Yoga, who haunts the stone trying to get it back. He sits on his heels in a corner of the room, digging in the floor with his hands, as of searching for it."

At some point, a friend convinced Heron-Allen to give her the stone. After much misfortune and disaster, she returned it to him. Deciding that enough was enough, Heron-Allen slung it into the Reagent's Canal. But the stone would not be stopped. Three months later, a dealer who had purchased the stone from a canal dredger brought the stone to Heron-Allen.

This time Heron-Allen gave it to a friend who was a singer. After accepting the stone, she found she could no longer sing, and returned the stone to him.

Cast it into the sea!
Worried that the stone's misfortune might affect his infant daughter, Heron-Allen packed it in seven boxes and deposited it in a safe deposit box at his bank "with directions that it is not to see the light again until I have been dead thirty three years." He stated that "Whoever shall open it, shall first read this warning, and then do so as he pleases with the Jewel." He advised the person opening the box to cast it into the sea, remarking that he was "forbidden by the Rosicrucian Oath to do this, or I would have done it long ago."

What a tale! It would make a great short story, and apparently it did.

According to a blog post on the Museum's web site examining the legend of the curse, "In fact, what is most likely is that Heron-Allen fabricated the legend to give credence to a short story he wrote in 1921 under the pseudonym Christopher Blayre, called 'The Purple Sapphire'."

Was the story written first, and the "evidence" written later to support it as the Museum blog suggests? Was he chronicling real events related to him by others? We'll probably never know.

The Hope Diamond
Cursed stone legends continue to fascinate us. Take the many cursed diamond tales to choose from. Probably the one we're most familiar with is that of the Hope Diamond. The first historical records suggest that a French merchant-traveler named Jean-Baptiste Tavernier obtained the stone in the mid-1600s. Some accounts say that he purchased the stone, which had been dug from the Kollur mine in Golconda, India. Others say that he stole it or had it stolen from a statue of the Hindu goddess Sita, and then was torn apart by wolves in Russia. This assertion contradicts the records saying he lived to 84, dying of natural causes.

If you analyze the fates of the succession of owners since Tavernier, there isn't a conclusive run of bad luck across the board. King Louis XIV and XV seemed not to suffer from the curse, though Louis XVI and Marie Antoinette were guillotined. Thomas Hope, for whom the diamond is named, was a man of the arts and lived a fruitful life as a life as a novelist and writer. French jeweler Pierre Cartier lived a prosperous life, dying at 86, though a

disagreement and resulting legal battle with the person who would subsequently buy the gem was heralded as evidence of the curse still being alive.

The Hope Diamond is a blue diamond. Traces of boron that give it this color are also responsible for an additional interesting characteristic: after it's exposed to short-wave ultraviolet light, the diamond produces a brilliant red phosphorescence. This strange red glow, which is not a normal property of diamonds, made it easier for people to believe the diamond possessed supernatural properties.

The Koh-i-Noor

Another cursed diamond, the Koh-i-Noor, also came from the Kollur Mine. It, too, originally graced a statue, but was stolen in the early 14th century, passing through the hands of many rulers. One, Nadir Shah, was assassinated. Upon his death the gem passed to his successors, two of whom were dethroned.

Almost one hundred years later, the then-owner of the stone, Maharaja Ranjit Singh, stated on his deathbed that he wished to donate the diamond to the Puri temple in Odisha. However, the British administrators did nothing at the time with the gem, and when the Punjab was formally proclaimed part of the British Company rule in India, the Koh-i-noor was surrendered to the Queen of England. On its way to England, the ship bearing the gem suffered an outbreak of cholera and then a severe gale that blew for twelve hours. Today a replica of the Koh-i-Noor is on display at the gallery's Vault Natural History Museum. The real gem is in the Tower Of London, part of the Crown Jewels, under armed guard.

The Black Orlov

Our final cursed diamond, the Black Orlov, was also stolen from a statue of a Hindu god, Brahma, in India and the theft caused it to be cursed. Also called the Eye of Brahma diamond, it took its later name from a Russian princess, Nadia Vyegin-Orlov. Like other cursed diamond legends, facts are disputed — one source says the Princess Nadia Vyegin-Orlov is wholly fictitious.

The Black Orlov is reputed to have caused the suicides of this princess, as well as another Russian royal, Princess Leonila Galitsine-Bariatinsky, both in 1947, and the suicide of J. W. Paris, the dealer who imported the stone to the United States fifteen years earlier.

Instead of packing it in seven boxes and depositing it in a safe deposit box at his bank, as Heron-Allen did with the cursed amethyst, the most-recent owners of the Black Orlov cut the stone in three, hoping to break the curse. So far this seems to have worked.

The Black Prince's Ruby

Another hard natural gem associated with a curse is the Black Prince's Ruby. Since the middle of the 14th century, rulers of England have owned this bauble, starting with its namesake, the "Black Prince" Edward of Woodstock. One of the oldest of the Crown Jewels of the United Kingdom, gemologically it's really a spinel, a singly refractive stone and not a true ruby, which is dichroic, but that doesn't hinder its power to curse.

Like the other precious gems mentioned so far, it was most likely mined in the Indian subcontinent. But instead of being plucked from the eye socket of a religious statue, this gem was pulled from the pocket of a murdered sultan by his murderer, King Pedro the Cruel.

The first manifestation of the curse was that Pedro soon found himself under attack from his half-brother. As remuneration for helping him repel his half-brother's attack, King Pedro gave the ruby to Prince Edward.

Edward's bad luck was that he died one year before his father, becoming the first English Prince of Wales not to become King of England. The stone passed to his son, King Richard II, who was later murdered by Henry IV. After his murder, the stone passed to Richard's son, King Henry V, who died of dysentery which he contracted during the siege of Meaux. After that, the curse resurfaced periodically but not consistently, and has lain relatively quiet for the past 300 years.

– MORVEN WESTFIELD

41

MOON GARDENING

BY PHASE

Sow, transplant, bud and graft		Plow, cultivate, weed and reap	

NEW	First Quarter	FULL	Last Quarter	NEW
Plant above-ground crops with outside seeds, flowering annuals.	Plant above-ground crops with inside seeds.	Plant root crops, bulbs, biennials, perennials.		Do not plant.

BY PLACE IN THE ZODIAC

Fruitful Signs

Cancer — Most favorable planting time for all leafy crops bearing fruit above ground. Prune to encourage growth in Cancer.

Scorpio — Second only to Cancer, a Scorpion Moon promises good germination and swift growth. In Scorpio, prune for bud development.

Pisces — Planting in the last of the Watery Triad is especially effective for root growth.

Taurus — The best time to plant root crops is when the Moon is in the sign of the Bull.

Capricorn — The Earthy Goat Moon promotes the growth of rhizomes, bulbs, roots, tubers and stalks. Prune now to strengthen branches.

Libra — Airy Libra may be the least beneficial of the Fruitful Signs, but is excellent for planting flowers and vines.

Barren Signs

Leo — Foremost of the Barren Signs, the Lion Moon is the best time to effectively destroy weeds and pests. Cultivate and till the soil.

Gemini — Harvest in the Airy Twins; gather herbs and roots. Reap when the Moon is in a sign of Air or Fire to assure best storage.

Virgo — Plow, cultivate, and control weeds and pests when the moon is in Virgo.

Sagittarius — Plow and cultivate the soil or harvest under the Archer Moon. Prune now to discourage growth.

Aquarius — This dry sign of Air is perfect for ground cultivation, reaping crops, gathering roots and herbs. It is a good time to destroy weeds and pests.

Aries — Cultivate, weed, and prune to lessen growth. Gather herbs and roots for storage.

Consult our Moon Calendar pages for phase and place in the zodiac circle. The Moon remains in a sign for about two-and-a-half days. Match your gardening activity to the day that follows the Moon's entry into that zodiac sign.

The MOON *Calendar*

is divided into zodiac signs rather than the more familiar Gregorian calendar.

2016

2017

Bear in mind that new projects should be initiated when the Moon is waxing (from dark to full). When the Moon is on the wane (from full to dark), it is a time for storing energy and the wise person waits.

Please note that Moons are listed by day of entry into each sign. Quarters are marked, but as rising and setting times vary from one region to another, it is advisable to check your local newspaper, library or planetarium.

The Moon's Place is computed for Eastern Standard Time.

Jewels of the Zodiac

THE BIRTHSTONES regarded today as traditional were actually assigned at a meeting of the National Association of Retail Jewelers in Kansas City in 1912. But although the correspondences seem based on commercialism and, in some instances, mere whimsy, investigation proves there was a random rhyme and reason for their choices.

The custom of adorning oneself with gems to complement the seasons had narrowed down to wearing of natal stones by the eighteenth century in Europe. Jewelers cast about for a proper source and not surprisingly chose the Bible. Two references, one each from the Old and New Testaments, served their purpose. The first was the description of the jewels in the breastplate of Aaron, high priest of the Jews, in Exodus 28:17–20. This soon proved unreliable, for the order and the translations of gem names were disputed then, as now, by Biblical scholars. The second, based on the listing of jewels adorning the wall of the New Jerusalem from the Apocalypse 21:19–20, seemed to be firmer ground and had already been successfully applied to other groups of twelve. In those days the year began in March, so the sequence was as follows: jasper, sapphire, chalcedony, emerald, sardonyx, sardius, chrysolite, beryl, topaz, chrysoprase, jacinth and amethyst. The Kansas City convention drew on the two Biblical sources,

borrowed from Arabic and Hindu traditions, and was influenced by a popular occult tome, *The Light of Egypt*. As these lists had been previously assigned to the zodiac signs, the shift to months caused odd transitions. It is clear that the birthstone scheme evolved more from accidental sequence than logical correspondences.

Agrippa's choice of zodiacal stones in his *On Occult Philosophy*, Volume II, is marked by the careful thought of a scholar and metaphysician. The birthstones according to Agrippa are:

Aries—SARDONYX
Taurus—CARNELIAN
Gemini—TOPAZ
Cancer—CHALCEDONY
Leo—JASPER
Virgo—EMERALD
Libra—BERYL
Scorpio—AMETHYST
Sagittarius—SAPPHIRE
Capricorn—CHYRSOPRASE
Aquarius—CRYSTAL
Pisces—LAPIS LAZULI

We researched the lore surrounding each jewel and separated Antonia Lamb's predictions for the sun signs ahead with tales about the gems Agrippa chose to correspond with them.

– Originally published in the 1975/1976 Witches' Almanac.

capricorn

December 21, 2015 – January 19, 2016

Cardinal Sign of Earth ▽ Ruled by Saturn ♄

S	M	T	W	T	F	S
	Dec. 21 Winter Solstice ❄ Taurus	22	23 Gemini	24 Howl at the moon	25 Wolf Moon Cancer	26 WANING
27 Watch the sun rise Leo	28	29 Rescue a pet	30 Austin Osman Spare born 1886 Virgo	31	Jan. 1 2016 Libra	2
3	4 Make a poppet Scorpio	5	6 Bonnie Franklin born 1944 Sagittarius	7 The Fates know	8 Feast of Janus ⇨ Capricorn	9
10 WAXING	11 Enjoy fine music Aquarius	12	13 Heal the sick Pisces	14	15 Beware of flames Aries	16
17 Taurus	18 Guard your treasures	19 Gemini				

SALAMANDER

The zoological salamander is an unremarkable little amphibian that resembles a lizard. But its mythological counter-part has a uniquely wondrous quality — a body so icy that it can withstand flames. Belief concerning the salamander's marvelous virtue existed in ancient Egypt and Babylon. In Greece, Aristotle wrote that the salamander "not only walks through fire, but puts it out in doing so."… A medieval monk kept the myth alive by recording: "This animal is the only one which puts the flames out. Indeed, it lives in the middle of the blaze without being hurt and without being burnt."

– excerpt from *The Little Book of Magical Creatures*

Celestial Gems

By consulting a wide spectrum of sources – ancient, classical, medieval, renaissance and modern – we've assembled a list of jewels most consistently linked with a particular heavenly body down through the centuries of Western occult tradition.

Agate – Mercury

Alexandrite – Mercury

Amber – Moon

Amethyst – Jupiter

Aquamarine – Venus

Beryl – Venus

Bloodstone – Mars

Carbuncle – Venus

Carnelian – Sun

Cat's Eye – Sun

Chalcedony – Saturn

Chrysoprase – Venus

Crystal – Moon

Diamond – Sun

Emerald – Venus

Garnet – Sun

Jacinth – Jupiter

Jade – Venus

Jasper – Mercury

Jet – Saturn

Lapis-lazuli – Jupiter

Malachite – Venus

Moonstone – Moon

Onyx – Saturn

Opal – Mercury

Pearl – Moon

Peridot – Venus

Quartz – Moon

Ruby – Mars

Sapphire – Jupiter

Sardonyx – Mercury

Topaz – Sun

Tourmaline – Mercury

Turquoise – Venus

aquarius

January 20 – February 18, 2016
Fixed Sign of Air ♎ Ruled by Uranus ♅

S	M	T	W	T	F	S
hawk *Early Egyptians, observing the bird's dominion of the airy realm, referred to it as "God of the Sky." They* (continued below)			Jan. 20	21 *Gregori Rasputin born 1869* Cancer	22	23 Storm Moon
24 WANING Leo	25	26 *Mind your health* Virgo	27	28 Libra	29 *Gather with friends*	30
31 ◑ Scorpio	Feb. 1 *Oimelc Eve*	2 *Candlemas* Sagittarius	3 *Focus your mind*	4	5 Capricorn	6 *Adam Weishaupt born 1748*
7 Year of the Monkey ⇨ Aquarius	8 ●	9 WAXING Pisces	10	11 *Exercise caution* Aries	12 *Dine with your beloved*	13 Taurus
14 Lupercalia ⇨	15 ◑ Gemini	16 *Show compassion*	17	18 Cancer		

named the hawk Horus and worshipped him before the dynasties began, believing that this bird's quality defined a vision of all that was worthy of respect and devotion. His right eye represented the Sun; his left, the Moon; the stars shone in his speckled plumage. Temple priests must have tamed and tended the wild birds, for they were depicted in ancient art perched on a block without tether, free to fly as they chose. – excerpt from *The Little Book of Magical Creatures*

≈ Bogeys ≈

IMPS RUN THE gamut from mischievous to harmful, but they do mortals the odd favor. Occasionally at dark of night imps sweep the floors or churn the butter. But bogeys are strangers to the milk of kindness. Both spirits are small but there the resemblance ends, for bogeys are scruffy, dress in raggedy clothes and have "meddling hands and clumsy feet." You know they are there by things that go bump in the night and the mishaps. Bogeys tip over bottles, scare cats, lame dogs, sour milk, pinch children, pull a person's ears. Sometimes they terrify sleepers by crawling into beds, patting faces with clammy hands and yanking off the covers.

The malicious little rascals are also known as "bogies," "boggarts," "boggles" and "boggards," frightening by any name. Their preferred turf is Britain, generally inhabiting houses or sometimes lonely places. In 1821 a Mrs. Wheeler described in a local Westmoreland paper, "Sic a terrible boggart as I beleev nivver onny yan saa befoar." Forty years later Cornhill Magazine quotes another spooked correspondent, "I darena come up the lone moor by night, for 'tis a very boggety bit."

A horseshoe nailed to a door is said to discourage their habitation, but once they find a home they dig in. The family must move by stealth, a moonlight flit, and pray that their bogey will never track them down. The expression "mind boggling," overcome with fear or astonishment, derives from bogeys and brings us to the horseshoe connection. An 1863 publication informs us about skittish horses, "When a horse takes fright at some object unobserved by its master, the vulgar [common] opinion is that it has seen the boggart."

Buried in the folklore, like a single raisin in a fruitcake, is actually one way to rid a house of this scourge. At heart the bogey is a dude, despite his tattered duds. If you make him a nice little suit that fits, he will grace you with his absence.

– BARBARA STACY

pisces
February 19 – March 20, 2016
Mutable Sign of Water ▽ *Ruled by Neptune* ♆

PISCES

S	M	T	W	T	F	S
		CHIMERA Chimera is another Greek mythological animal you don't want to chance meeting, not even in your (continued below)			Feb. 19	20 Leo
21	22 Chaste Moon Virgo	23 WANING	24 Giovanni Mirandola born 1463	25 Libra	26 A new birth	27 Scorpio
28 Gamble just a little	29 Leap Year Day	March 1 Sagittarius	2 Matronalia ⇐	3 Capricorn	4 Play games of chance	5 Aquarius
6	7 Total solar eclipse ⇒	8 Pisces	9 WAXING	10 Start a new project Aries	11	12 Taurus
13 Robert Felkin born 1853	14 Gemini	15	16 Cancer	17 Hold tight	18 Leo	19 Minerva's Day

20 · dreams. The beast would be easy enough to recognize, having the head of a lion, the torso of a goat, and the tail of a serpent... the chimera has a fiery breath that sizzles to a crisp anything within range except the odd hero. Homer tells us that "Her pitchy nostrils flaky flames expire; / Her gaping throat emits infernal fire."

– excerpt from The Little Book of Magical Creatures

49

Witches concocting an ointment to be used for flying to the Sabbath.
Hans Baldung Grien, Strassburg, 1514

THIS ALSO is not to be omitted, that certain wicked women, turned back toward Satan, seduced by demonic illusions and phantasms, believe of themselves and profess to ride upon certain beasts in the nighttime hours, with Diana, the Goddess of the Pagans, and an innumerable multitude of women, and to traverse great spaces of earth in the silence of the dead of night, and to be subject to her laws as of a Lady, and on fixed nights be called to her service.

– Heresy in the Roman Catholic Church: A History
Michael C. Thomsett

aries

March 20 – April 19, 2016

Cardinal Sign of Fire △ Ruled by Mars ♂

S	M	T	W	T	F	S
Mar. 20 2016 Vernal Equinox Leo	21 Virgo	22 Partial lunar eclipse ⇨	23 Seed Moon Libra	24 WANING	25	26 Scorpio
27	28 Sagittarius	29 Pearl Bailey born 1918	30	31 Capricorn	April 1 All Fools' Day	2 Aquarius
3 Practice meditation	4 Too many secrets Pisces	5	6 Move Forward Aries	7	8 WAXING Taurus	9
10 Gemini	11	12 Plant indoors Cancer	13	14 Leo	15 Bessie Smith born 1898	16
17 Virgo	18	19 Wear red Libra				

Minerva – March 19: Minerva was identified with the Greek Athena, the patron of arts, crafts and professions, protector of cities, inspirer of with and resourceful action, her symbol the owl. Guilds and craftsmen, actors and poets met in her temple. But despite her wisdom, Minerva was as wildly jealous and vindictive as all the deities when their powers were challenged.

– BARBARA STACY, *Ancient Roman Holidays*

HERBALISTS' SYMBOLS

✠

Symbol	Meaning	Symbol	Meaning
ℳ.ℹ.	pound	Σ	sugar
ANA	equal amounts		alcohol
℥.ℹ.	ounce		honey
℈.ℹ.	dram		mix
℈.ℹ.	scruple		boil
P.ℹ.	pinch	℞	take
⊘.ℹ.	pint		distill
	still	◇	filter
	retort		essence
	receiver		powder
	vinegar		compose

taurus
April 20 – May 20, 2016
Fixed Sign of Earth ♒ Ruled by Venus ♀

S	M	T	W	T	F	S
			APRIL 20	21 Earth Day ⇨	22 Hare Moon	23 *Plant seeds* Scorpio
24 WANING Sagittarius	25	26 *Marcus Aurelius born 121*	27 *Fools rush in* Capricorn	28	29 Aquarius	30 *Walpurgis Night*
MAY 1 Beltane Pisces	2 *Gather dew*	3 Aries	4	5 *Leave offerings at an oak* Taurus	6	7 WAXING Gemini
8 White Lotus Day	9 Cancer	10	11 *Salvador Dali born 1904* Leo	12	13 Virgo	14
15 *Greet the Sun*	16 Libra	17 WAXING	18	19 *Meet your love at night* Scorpio	20 Vesak Day	

Nefer: This is an ancient Egyptian amulet made in the form of a stringed musical instrument. It was always red, made of carnelian or some semiprecious red stone or red porcelain. The nefer is believed to bring its wearer good luck and happiness. The amulet, which enjoyed extreme popularity, was usually strung with beads on a necklace or worn alone as a pendant.

– ELIZABETH PEPPER, *Magic Charms from A to Z*

AIR

Do not worry if you have built your castles in the air. They are where they should be. Now put the foundations under them.
— *Henry David Thoreau*

A boy's will is the wind's will,
And the thoughts of youth are long, long thoughts.
— *Longfellow*

The pessimist complains about the wind; the optimist expects it to change; the realist adjusts the sails.
— *William Arthur Ward*

Kites rise highest against the wind — not with it.
— *Winston Churchill*

The desire to fly is an idea handed down to us by our ancestors who... looked enviously on the birds soaring freely through space... on the infinite highway of the air.
— *Wilbur Wright*

Come Fairies, take me out of this dull world, for I would ride with you upon the wind and dance upon the mountains like a flame!
— *William Butler Yeats*

For what is it to die, But to stand in the sun and melt into the wind?
— *Kahlil Gibran*

Adversity is like a strong wind. It tears away from us all but the things that cannot be torn, so that we see ourselves as we really are.
— *Arthur Golden*

If you surrendered to the air, you could ride it.
— *Toni Morrison*

Quotes compiled by Isabel Kunkle.

gemini

May 21 – June 20, 2016

Mutable Sign of Air ♎ Ruled by Mercury ☿

S	M	T	W	T	F	S
			The Moon and the Sun; Although the semicircle of the Moon is placed above the circle of the Sun and would appear to be superior, nevertheless *(continued below)*			MAY 21 Dyad Moon Sagittarius
22 WANING	23 *Sing a song of love*	24 Capricorn	25 *Miles Davis born 1926*	26 Aquarius	27	28 *Trust in your friends*
29 Pisces	30 Oak Apple ⇐Day	31 *Avoid conflict* Aries	JUNE 1	2 Taurus	3 *Share your love*	4 Gemini
5 WAXING	6 Night ⇐ of the Watchers Cancer	7	8 Leo	9 *Return a favor*	10 Virgo	11 *Richard Strauss born 1864*
12 Libra	13	14	15 *Carry Bloodstone* Scorpio	16	17	18 *Greet the birds* Sagittarius
19 *Esbat Circle*	20 Rose Moon	we know that the Sun is ruler and King. We see that the Moon in her shape and her proximity rivals the Sun with her grandeur, which is apparent to ordinary men, yet the face, or a semi-sphere of the Moon, always reflects the light of the Sun. – JOHN DEE, *Monas Hieroglyphica*				

FULL MOON NAMES

STUDENTS OF OCCULT literature soon learn the importance of names. From Ra to Rumpelstiltskin, the message is clear—names hold unusual power.

The tradition of naming full Moons was recorded in an English edition of The *Shepherd's Calendar*, published in the first decade of the 16th century.

Aries—Seed. Sowing season and symbol of the start of the new year.

Taurus—Hare. The sacred animal was associated in Roman legends with springtime and fertility.

Gemini—Dyad. The Latin word for a pair refers to the twin stars of the constellation Castor and Pollux.

Cancer—Mead. During late June and most of July the meadows, or meads, were mowed for hay.

Leo—Wort. When the sun was in Leo the worts (from the Anglo-Saxon wyrt-plant) were gathered to be dried and stored.

Virgo — Barley. Persephone, virgin goddess of rebirth, carries a sheaf of barley as symbol of the harvest.

Libra — Blood. Marking the season when domestic animals were sacrificed for winter provisions.

Scorpio — Snow. Scorpio heralds the dark season when the Sun is at its lowest and the first snow flies.

Sagittarius—Oak. The sacred tree of the Druids and the Roman god Jupiter is most noble as it withstands winter's blasts.

Capricorn — Wolf. The fearsome nocturnal animal represents the "night" of the year. Wolves were rarely seen in England after the 12th century.

Aquarius — Storm. A storm is said to rage most fiercely just before it ends, and the year usually follows suit.

Pisces — Chaste. The antiquated word for pure reflects the custom of greeting the new year with a clear soul.

Libra's Full Moon occasionally became the Wine Moon when a grape harvest was expected to produce a superior vintage.

America's early settlers continued to name the full Moons. The influence of the native tribes and their traditions is readily apparent.

AMERICAN	COLONIAL	NATIVE
Aries / April	Pink, Grass, Egg	Green Grass
Taurus / May	Flower, Planting	Shed
Gemini / June	Rose, Strawberry	Rose, Make Fat
Cancer / July	Buck, Thunder	Thunder
Leo / August	Sturgeon, Grain	Cherries Ripen
Virgo / September	Harvest, Fruit	Hunting
Libra / October	Hunter's	Falling Leaf
Scorpio / November	Beaver, Frosty	Mad
Sagittarius / December	Cold, Long Night	Long Night
Capricorn / January	Wolf, After Yule	Snow
Aquarius / February	Snow, Hunger	Hunger
Pisces / March	Worm, Sap, Crow	Crow, Sore Eye

cancer
June 21 – July 22, 2016
Cardinal Sign of Water ▽ Ruled by Moon ☽

S	M	T	W	T	F	S
		JUNE 21 Summer Solstice ☼ Capricorn	22 WANING	23 Aquarius	24 Midsummer	25 Gather St. Johnswort Pisces
26	27 Aries	28	29 Taurus	30 Buddy Rich born 1917	JULY 1 Gemini	2 Study the birds
3 Cancer	4	5 WAXING Leo	6 Welcome a stranger	7	8 Walk the path Virgo	9 Maintain balance
10 Libra	11	12 Oscar Hammerstein born 1895	13 Scorpio	14 Embrace change	15 Sagittarius	16
17 Kiss the Moon	18 Light the cauldron Capricorn	19 Mead Moon	20 WANING Aquarius	21	22 Visit the sea Pisces	

Heather: Heather now joins furze, adding great patches of white, pin and mauve flowers to the countryside's splendor; a visual tribute to Summer Solstice.
At Midsummer, the longest day of the year, the sun reaches the height of its power. Heather thrives in full sun and blooms through Autumn.

– CELTIC TREE MAGIC

The Turtle and the Eagle

A TURTLE saw an eagle flying and thought that he would like to fly also. The turtle offered the eagle money to teach him how. The eagle said it was impossible, but the turtle kept on pleading and insisting. So the eagle picked him up and flew into the sky. When they were very high up, the eagle let go of the turtle, who landed on a rock and was killed.

Moral: Trying for things that are impossible may lead to disaster.

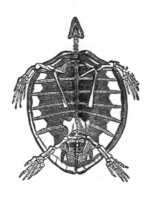

leo

July 23 – August 22, 2016

Fixed Sign of Fire △ Ruled by Sun ☉

S	M	T	W	T	F	S
The Wise Ones: The wise ones serve on the higher, but rule on the lower. They obey the laws coming from above them, but on their own plane, and those below them they rule and give orders. And, yet, in so doing, they form a part of the Principle, instead of opposing it. The wise man falls in with the Law, and by understanding its movements he operates it instead of being its blind slave. Just as does the skilled *(continued below)*						**JULY 23** Ancient Egyptian New Year
24 Ruth Buzzi born, 1936 Aries	**25**	**26** ◑ Taurus	**27**	**28** Tame your wild side Gemini	**29**	**30** Bake bread
31 Lughnassad Eve Cancer	**AUGUST 1** Lammas 🐝	**2** ● Leo	**3** WAXING	**4** Virgo	**5**	**6** Run through a meadow Libra
7	**8**	**9** Scorpio	**10** ◐	**11** Sagittarius	**12** Harvest maze	**13** Diana's Day
14 Capricorn	**15** Napoleon Bonaparte born 1769	**16** Aquarius	**17** Black Cat Appreciation Day	**18** ◯ Wort Moon	**19** Partial lunar ⇐ eclipse Pisces	**20** WANING
21 Aries	**22** Gaze into a candle flame	swimmer turn this way and that way, going and coming as he will, instead of being as the log which is carried here and there — so is the wise man as compared to the ordinary man — and yet both swimmer and log; wise man and fool, are subject to Law. He who understands this is well on the road to Mastery. – THE KYBALION				

59

Memoir

The Amber Leaf

A LITTLE Chinese treasure box. It is two inches square, of gold brocade flecked with tiny flowers and fastened with a tiny spear of ivory that slides into a loop. On the white silk lining rests a small amber leaf. It is a good-luck charm, a present from a woman of power, who assured me that it would bring good luck and strength. I have kept it for thirty years, lying in its little silk nest and removed occasionally to be rubbed, as instructed, to activate the magic. Perhaps I believe in such mystique, perhaps not. But an eighty-year-old friend has been going through hospital hell, and I have passed it along to him. I think he has no belief in anything much beyond love of his wife and yet he says that the little leaf gave him comfort. Maybe the little amber leaf wafted magic. Maybe it wafted the power of human affinity. Maybe it's just a little amber leaf, signifying nothing.

– Barbara Stacy

virgo

August 23 – September 21, 2016

Mutable Sign of Earth ▽ Ruled by Mercury ☿

S	M	T	W	T	F	S
		AUG. **23** Taurus	**24** Gemini	**25** Gemini	**26**	**27** Cancer
28	**29** *Ingrid Bergman born 1915* Leo	**30** *Bathe in darkness*	**31** Partial solar eclipse ⇨ Virgo	SEPT. **1**	**2** WAXING	**3** Libra
4 *Cherish today*	**5** Ganesh Festival Scorpio	**6** *Record your dreams*	**7**	**8** *Peter Sellers born 1925* Sagittarius	**9**	**10** Capricorn
11	**12** *Challenge yourself*	**13** Aquarius	**14**	**15** Partial lunar eclipse ⇨ Pisces	**16** Barley Moon	**17** WANING Aries
18 *Find north*	**19**	**20**	**21** *Collect a fallen feather* Gemini			

To the West Wind (Zephyros): The Fumigation from Frankincense. Sea-born, aerial, blowing from the west, sweet gales [Aurai], who give to weary'd labour rest: Vernal and grassy, and of gentle found, to ships delightful, thro' the sea profound; For these, impell'd by you with gentle force, pursue with prosp'rous Fate their destin'd course. With blameless gales regard my suppliant pray'r, Zephyrs unseen, light-wing'd, and form'd from air. — ORPHIC HYMN 80

TAROT'S HANGED MAN

THE HANGED MAN dangles precariously from one leg, crucified on a living cross. The ground is nowhere in sight. Surely his is a desperate situation. But, like many stops on the Fool's journey, number twelve of the Major Arcana is not as it first appears. Look closer at the man's face and notice an expression free of pain. In fact, his countenance is serene, unperturbed and perhaps even liberated by his current predicament. His hands rest patiently behind his back, not clawing desperately at his tether. His free leg rests easily, almost casually crossed behind its ensnared twin. His head radiates a golden crown of Divine enlightenment. In sacrificing his physical comfort and mobility, The Hanged Man has gained spiritual clarity.

The Hanged Man calls for a suspension of activity, a period of reflection and deep examinations, a dwelling in the present moment. It implores the querent to challenge preconceived convictions and become open to new possibilities through self-sacrifice and surrendering to uncertainty. Gaining perspective outside oneself can be tricky, inclined as we are to see what we want to see. Flipping the world upside can be an effective treatment for this inherent confirmation bias. While you may not need to go as far as literally hanging upside down to gain a new perspective, you will have to be willing to make yourself uncomfortable. Enlightenment will not come easily.

libra

September 22 – October 22, 2016

Cardinal Sign of Air ♎ Ruled by Venus ♀

LIBRA

S	M	T	W	T	F	S
Aten – the God of the Sky: If this were a new religion, invented to satisfy our modern scientific conceptions, we could not find a flaw in the correctness of this view of the energy of the solar system. How much Akhenaten understood, we cannot say, but *(continued below)*				**Sept. 22** Autumnal Equinox ♌	**23** Cancer	**24**
25 Indulge yourself Leo	**26**	**27** Endure	**28** Virgo	**29** Enrico Fermi born 1901	**30** Libra	**Oct. 1** WAXING
2	**3** Watch your temper Scorpio	**4**	**5** Be evasive Sagittarius	**6**	**7**	**8** Gather oak leaves Capricorn
9 Aquarius	**10**	**11** Write a letter	**12** Pisces	**13**	**14** Richard Cromwell born 1626 Aries	**15**
16 Blood Moon Taurus	**17** WANING	**18** Gemini	**19**	**20** Gather ancestor photos Cancer	**21**	**22**

he certainly bounded forward in his views and symbolism to a position which we cannot logically improve upon at the present day. Not a rag of superstition or of falsity can be found clinging to this new worship evolved out of the old Aton of Heliopolis, the sole Lord of the universe.

– FLINDERS PETRIE, 1899

Over the floor
And down the wall,
Like ghosts
The shadows rise and fall!

– Excerpt from *The Sleeper*
by Edgar Allan Poe

scorpio
October 23 – November 21, 2016
Fixed Sign of Water ▽ Ruled by Pluto ♀

S	M	T	W	T	F	S
Oct. 23 Leo	24 Prepare a brew	25 Virgo	26	27 Theodore Roosevelt born 1858 Libra	28	29
30 ● Scorpio	31 Samhain Eve WAXING	Nov. 1 Hallowmas Sagittarius	2 Visit a grave	3	4 Love what you lost Capricorn	5
6 Aquarius	7 ◐	8 Pisces	9 Mary A. Travers born 1936	10 Cleanse your home	11 Aries	12
13 Taurus	14 ◯ Snow Moon	15 WANING Gemini	16 Hecate Night	17 Saturnalia Cancer	18	19 Guide by instinct Leo
20	21 ◑ Virgo					

The Four Winds: Now the pyre of dead Patroclus would not burn Fleet-footed Achilles took thought, then standing back from the pyre prayed to the winds, Boreas the North wind, Zephyrus the West, promising them fine offerings. Pouring libations from a golden cup, he begged them fervently to blow, so the wood might kindle and the bodies might burn. Iris heard his prayer, and flew swiftly to give the Winds his message. They were feasting together in Zephyrus' house, Lord of the Western Gales, when Iris halted on his stone threshold. They sprang up when they saw her, and called her to sit beside them. But she refused, saying: 'I can't, I must return to Ocean's stream, and the land of the Ethiopians, where they are sacrificing to the immortals, and share in their sacred feast. But Achilles asks for you Boreas, and you wild Zephyrus, and promises fine offerings if you'll kindle the pyre where Patroclus lies, for whom the Achaeans grieve.' – HOMER, *the Iliad Book XXIII*

The Eve of the Fairy Queen

Radiance on a bleak winter night

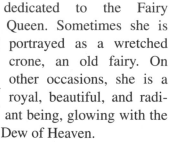

THE ANNUAL appearance on our Moon Calendar of Fairy Queen Eve, celebrated on December 16, has evoked the curiosity of those readers more familiar with seasonal Yuletide and Saturnalia celebrations. Numerous requests have been made for an explanation of this fey holiday, as well as for information on how to honor the occasion.

Fairy Queen Eve can be celebrated on many levels, true of many passages linked with the Old Ways. The days leading to the Winter Solstice mark a cycle when the gates to Fairyland, the Other World, are more accessible to mortals. A Celtic tradition exists with a connection to Queen Maeve (or Medb), who presides over her court, directing the preparations for the cross-quarter day of Yule, with its longest of nights.

The date specifically marks the beginning of a nine-day period of grace and waiting in early Catholic rituals dedicated to the Blessed Virgin Mary, Queen of the Universe. A time of reverie, of sacred anticipation, begins at 4 a.m. on December 16. For nine successive mornings, until Christmas Day, the enigmatic energies of a pre-dawn mass are dedicated to the Fairy Queen. Sometimes she is portrayed as a wretched crone, an old fairy. On other occasions, she is a royal, beautiful, and radiant being, glowing with the Dew of Heaven.

Fairy Queen Eve, among the holiest times of joy and penance, is now most familiar in the traditional Catholic cultures of the Philippines and Puerto Rico. December 16 is the start of the mass or *Misa de Aguinaldo*. *Aguinaldo* is a Spanish word meaning "a unique holiday gift." In Puerto Rico, this mass is completely musical and the *Aguinaldo* becomes the gift of holiday songs.

To call in the Fairy Queen, whether you see her as Maeve or Mary, withered or youthful, obtain a bell and a snow-white or silver-gilt candle. During the dark hours on December 16, ring the bell nine times and light the candle. Ask for her blessing. Be observant, for either the old woman or the lovely lady will probably appear to you. Most likely this will be briefly and from a distance, as you round a corner, during an outing, before Midwinter's day has passed.

– DANA N.

This Fairy Queen Eve feature is dedicated to the memory of Nadya, dear familiar and best friend, who, once upon a time, incarnated in this world on a Fairy Queen Eve.) – A.T.

sagittarius

November 22 – December 20, 2016

Mutable Sign of Fire △ Ruled by Jupiter ♃

S	M	T	W	T	F	S
		Nov. 22	23	24 William F. Buckley born 1925 Libra	25 Make no decisions	26 Scorpio
27	28 Seek kindred spirits	29 ● Sagittarius	30 WAXING	Dec. 1 Pray in the owl hour Capricorn	2 Offer love	3
4 Aquarius	5	6 Avoid conflict Pisces	7 ◑	8 David Carradine born 1936 Aries	9	10 Taurus
11 Befriend a small creature	12 Gemini	13 ○ Oak Moon	14 WANING Cancer	15	16 Lucky Day Leo	17 Fairy Queen Eve
18	19 Virgo	20 ◐				

Vayu and Brahman: He (Vayu) rushed to the Yaksha and Brahman asked him who he was. Replied Vayu, "I am Vayu. I am really the master of all skies." And Brahman enquired, "What is the nature of your power in you." And replied Vayu, "All this, whatever that is here, I can blow away." Brahman placed before him a blade of grass saying, "Blow it away." Vayu approached it with his full might, but could not move it even a little. He too returned to the gods saying, "I could not find that which this Spirit is."

– Kena Upanishad

Dear Santa Claus,

A timeless letter

"YES, VIRGINIA," as the famous letter, published in The New York Times over a century ago, read, "there is a Santa Claus." For the next fifty years, Virginia O'Hanlon, who at eight years old wrote the letter asking if Santa Claus was real, reread and commented on the editor's response. Santa Claus defined her entire life.

The message is that Santa arrives each winter to brighten the cold and the dark, rekindling the spirit of humor, hope, love and joy within humanity. Father Time didn't always appear as a rotund figure dressed in cheerful red, running a toy shop in the North Pole staffed by elves. The beloved patron of Yuletide and the Christmas season has evolved over centuries, but his actual origin is unidentifiable, lost in the most distant mists of time.

Santa is a hybrid descended from Saint Nicholas. His elven companions and flying sleigh may have been inspired by the Nordic deity, Odin. Perhaps his eight reindeer are tamer versions of Cernunnos, a Celtic stag god, who personifies the forces of masculinity.

The ancient winter festival of Saturnalia hints that today's kindly Santa is actually stern Saturn in disguise, bringing a warning about the consequences of not being nice. The Saturnalia was presided over by the Lord of Misrule, a vaguely Santa-like jester figure. He brought humor during the cold and snow of Yuletides long past.

Today's Santa Claus, chuckling the popular greeting "Merry Christmas," has emerged from the writings of Washington Irving, Thomas Pintard and Clement Clarke Moore, the author of *The Night Before Christmas*. Illustrator Thomas Nast was the first to portray our modern Santa.

Santa has appeared year-round in Coca Cola ads, since the 1930s. The soft drink company was seeking a way to boost its sales during their slow winter season. Haddon Sundblom, a gifted and imaginative artist, drew upon familiar images of Santa from *The Saturday Evening Post*, as well as Frances Hodgson Burnett's bestselling children's book, *Saint Nicholas*. The magic worked. With Santa as spokesperson, the year round sales of Coke skyrocketed like that magic sleigh on Christmas Eve.

Like church bells, Santa's sleigh bells are related to a traditional belief that sacred sound will drive away evil forces, while simultaneously calling out to the angelic realms for care and attention. The bells remain as noise makers through New Year's Eve to eliminate any bad situations and demons lingering from the year past. Appreciation of friends, ourselves and a promise of warmer, easier times to come is Santa's most precious gift of all.

– MARINA BRYONY

capricorn

December 21, 2016 – January 19, 2017

Cardinal Sign of Earth ♁ Ruled by Saturn ♄

S	M	T	W	T	F	S
			DEC. 21 Winter Solstice ❄ Libra	22 Praise Mistletoe	23 Scorpio	24 Observe an old custom
25 Little Richard born 1935	26 Sagittarius	27	28 Cast a spell Capricorn	29 ●	30 WAXING	31 Aquarius
JAN. 1 2017	2 Weather the storm Pisces	3	4 Aries	5 ◑	6 Taurus	7 Plan for the New Year
8 Light a candle	9 Feast of Janus Gemini	10 Find your answer	11 Cancer	12 Wolf Moon	13 WANING Leo	14 Surrender to love
15 Virgo	16	17 Muhammed Ali born, 1942 Libra	18 Bite your tongue	19 ◐		

Of Spells: The recitation of spells and charms should be at a tempo much slower than ordinary speech. We are told that the effect should be one of quite emphasis and certain intent. Some say that the sound should be loud and clear; others recommend a whisper. Another source insists that the words be musically intoned.

– ELIZABETH PEPPER, *Magic Spells and Incantations*

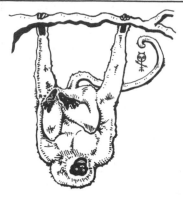

YEAR OF THE FIRE MONKEY
February 8, 2016 – January 27, 2017

THE WORLD'S oldest-known astrological system, the Chinese zodiac, in use for almost five millennia, is based on a twelve year cycle, rather than twelve months. Legend says that Buddha planned a party, inviting the animals to celebrate. Each of the twelve who attended was rewarded with a year. Buddha also decreed that each animal would hide within the hearts of individuals and events born during their year. The Chinese zodiac incorporates five elements (fire, water, metal, earth and wood). Every sixty years, paired animals and elements repeat.

Chinese New Year is celebrated at the second new moon after Winter Solstice. Those born early in the year — January Capricorns, as well as some Aquarians — may fall under the previous year's sign.

Witty, good-humored Monkey was the ninth to arrive at Buddha's gathering. Charming but contradictory, Monkey is candid and astute, yet also capable of guile and chicanery. Monkey finds ways to restore order amid chaos. The most human and intelligent of all animals, Monkey enjoys puzzles that challenge its agile mind and appreciates a good joke or intriguing tale.

The Year of the Fire Monkey favors originality and clear communication. Brainstorming sessions can be especially rewarding. Since monkeys tend to be strong, healthy animals, there may be general improvements regarding health.

An especially dynamic cycle begins for those born in Monkey years. Constructive efforts move forward. Exciting plans for the future begin to manifest. Be imaginative. A touch of wizardry is afoot.

More information on the Fire Monkey can be found on our website at http://The WitchesAlmanac.com/AlmanacExtras/.

Years of the Monkey
1932, 1944, 1956, 1968, 1980, 1992, 2004, 2016

Illustration by Ogmios MacMerlin

aquarius

January 20 – February 18, 2017

Fixed Sign of Air ♎ Ruled by Uranus ♅

S	M	T	W	T	F	S
♥	♥	♥	♥	♥	JAN. 20 Scorpio	21
22 Sagittarius	23 Beware of Jack Frost	24 Louis de Wohl born 1903	25 Capricorn	26 Gaze into a black mirror	27 ● Aquarius	28 Year of the Rooster
29 WAXING Pisces	30	31 Make an offering	FEB. 1 Oimelc Eve Aries	2 Candlemas	3 ◑ Taurus	4
5 Gemini	6 Make an incense	7 Cancer	8 Read the tarot	9 Partial lunar eclipse ⇨ Leo	10 Storm Moon	11 WANING Virgo
12 Place silver against gold	13	14 Jimmy Hoffa born 1913 Libra	15 Lupercalia	16 Scorpio	17 Use ginger root	18 ◐

Truth: Truth must be loved for its own sake. Those who speak the truth because they are in some way compelled to or for their own advantage, and who are not afraid to tell a lie when it is of no importance to anyone, is not truthful enough. My soul naturally shuns a lie, and hates even the thought of one. I feel an inward shame and a sharp remorse if an untruth happens to escape me — as sometimes it does if the occasion is unexpected, and I am taken unawares.
— MICHEL DE MONTAIGNE

Castles in the Sand

WHAT IS IT about castles that appeal to our collective imagination? Our childhood storybooks are filled with images of them — stone fortresses built high on mountain tops or hidden deep in enchanted forests. Most castles come ready-made with a resident king or queen, hopefully kind and generous folks, quick to declare a public celebration at the drop of a crown. In the more romantic tales, perhaps a beautiful prince or handsome princess graces the palace. As adults we perpetuate our fascination with castles by passing on the stories to our own children.

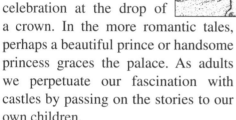

Nowhere is the mystery and allure of castles more visible than at the beach. Just go to any shoreline on a hot summer day and watch the children play at the water's edge. Some of them prefer to build their monuments out of sand. The secret to a formidable sand castle is in the water. Children go back and forth from the sea, carrying plastic buckets of foamy surf to the beach, where it is dumped out onto the sand and carefully mixed to the right consistency before becoming mortar for the strongest walls.

Other more enterprising children build their treasures out of rocks, scanning the beach to find just the right stones. They work at the castles for hours, just above the high tide line, sometimes alone, but more often in teams. Often these teams come together from different families. One child sees another struggling with construction of a wall and comes to help without being asked.

I stayed late at the beach one day to see what would happen when the water rose high enough to take down the castles of sand and stone. Some of the children had already left, packed into cars early by anxious parents along with beach umbrellas and soggy towels.

The children who remained to witness the inevitable surprised me with their courage. There were no tears or tantrums as the tide tore at the meticulous walls or broke through the most strategically stacked rocks. Instead there were smiles, even laughter. One child did a little happy dance to see her hours of labor destroyed by a single rush of water.

According to an article in *Psychology Today*, written by a well-respected child psychologist, sand castles are a "psychologically devastating reminder of the ubiquity of loss and the ephemeral nature of existence." Perhaps it's a lot less complex. Maybe it's not the castle itself that is important, but the fun one has in creating it, as well as deliriously inexplicable joy experienced when one realizes that they get to do it all again tomorrow.

– JIMAHL DI FIOSA

pisces

February 19 – March 20, 2017

Mutable Sign of Water ▽ Ruled by Neptune ♆

S	M	T	W	T	F	S
Feb. 19 *Nicholas Copernicus born 1473* Sagittarius	20	21 Capricorn	22 *Call a friend*	23 Aquarius	24 *Eat a sweet*	25
26 ● Pisces	27 Partial solar ⇦ eclipse	28 WAXING Aries	March 1 Matronalia	2 Taurus	3 *Buy seeds*	4 Gemini
5 ◐ Cancer	6 *Dream of roses*	7	8 *Syd Charisse born 1922* Leo	9	10	11 *Plan your garden* Virgo
12 Chaste Moon	13 Libra	14 WANING	15 *Meditate on the Moon* Scorpio	16 *Search the sky*	17	18 Sagittarius
19 Minerva's Day	20 ◐ Capricorn					

Stronger, Happier, Wiser: No changing of place at a hundred miles an hour will make us one whit stronger, or happier, or wiser. There was always more in the world than we could see, walked we ever so slowly; we will see it no better for going fast. The really precious things are thought and sight, not pace. It does a bullet no good to go fast; and a person, if he or she be truly a man or woman, no harm to go slow; for our glory is not at all in going, but in being. — JOHN RUSKIN

Deosil and Widdershins

Celestial power from the sun's path

IF YOU DON'T KNOW which way to turn, allow the Sun's course to aid you in ritual circles. Wise ones have been doing the same since time immemorial, codifying discoveries and attuning to the Sun's travel through the heavens. In the broadest view, a circle symbolizes the completion of a cycle of existence, the eternal return, perpetual motion, continuity through time, clockwork. The symbol in all its complexity is simple to draw and widely applied in ritual, often for protection. Inside the ring lies the realm of magic, performance of a sacred rite. Outside lies the material world, containing evil forces and all kinds of unruly spirits, as well as a realm that might be influenced by the powers conjured within the circle.

The size of the circle may be widely varied and used in widely varied ways. The form may be created in boulders, pebbles, salt or chalk. Inside the ring may be a solitary witch, a coven or other group, perhaps for healing, expanding capacity as necessary. The ceremony may include an altar and tools, and offer invocations to deities, singing, dancing, drumming, scents, herbs, spells, divination, auguries, potions, any number of devices. Often a circle of celebration occurs on holidays and special occasions.

Deosil and widdershins describe the two classical approaches to ceremonial working with circles. In their most basic forms, deosil is clockwise around the Sun, east to west, to the right if circling an object. This motion is perceived as a positive force, drawing in energy from the Sun, perhaps relating to the right hand bias of many cultures. Widdershins refers to counterclockwise, west to east, skewed left for circles and considered unlucky, "against the Sun," especially by early Sun-worship cultures. (Alert readers will immediately note that the directions apply only to the Northern Hemisphere and the opposite prevails in the Southern.)

The roundabout words themselves clue us into old beliefs. "Deosil" derives from Irish-Gaelic and its first syllable has nothing to do with god. The "deo" refers to deum, meaning "day" and refers to the Sun. Oddly enough deosil is pronounced JEE-zhel — yes, go figure Gaelic pronunciation. "Widdershins" was first cited in 1513 from widdersyns, "start my hair," meaning "my hair stood on end," a good description of some responses to left hand movement. The root is German, *wittersinnig*, "against sense," also interpreted as "opposite the usual."

Signifying

Stone dolmen circles from the Megalith Era reveal the antiquity of the symbol. Doubtless built as burial sites, perhaps the ring of boulders such as Stonehenge provided protection for the deceased and also a site for memorial rites. We know that the earliest Pagans worshipped within groves and sought to build their altars where trees formed a ring.

We have no record of when the deosil/widdershins distinctions began, but the druids knew. They took advantage of the knowledge in their circumnavigation ceremonies, walking around their temples from the south and keeping the structure on the right. This course they believed propitious; the contrary path, *tuathal*, fatal or at least ominous. In Britain, it was considered unlucky even for travelers to pass widdershins around a church. In the folk tale, "Childe Rowland," the protagonist and his sister are carried off to Elfland after she runs counterclockwise around a churchyard.

But two Asian religions at the same site differ on approaches to shrines. Tibetan Buddhists go around deosil, while followers of Bonpo go widdershins. Tibetan monks consider the Bonpo usage a perversion of right practice. The Bonpo adherents claim that since they are the native population of Tibet, their practice is definitive.

Some Jewish traditions also vary. In the synagogue, as the Torah is removed from the Ark for reading, the scroll is taken from the right and returned on the left. At a wedding, the bride circles the groom seven times widdershins. Dancers on all occasions also circle in that direction. Fortunately the dancing tends to take place indoors — according to one myth, if you dance nine times around a ring of toadstools you will come under the power of the fairy kingdom. Imagine the shock!

Circling the globe

In folk tales, wherever imagination sparkles and stories are born, circles pop up as magical devices. *Szepasszony*

Talmudic literature contains several stories about using circles to make rain. Choni the Circle, also known as Choni the Rainmaker, offers a droll example of the power of piety. In his day, the second century BCE, a drought blighted Israel, despite the best efforts of the rabbis to enact prayer vigils. As spring approached, they decided to call on the legendary rainmaker, famous for his close relationship to God.

Choni drew a circle, stood inside, and said, "Master of the Universe, Your children have turned their faces to me, for I am like a member of Your household. I swear by Your great Name that I will not move from here until You have mercy on Your children."

Rain spattered down in droplets. "I did not ask this," Choni pointed out, and asked for more rain. More came down angrily in torrents. "I did not ask this," Choni persisted, "but rains of benevolence, blessing and generosity." The torrent abated and such rains fell as saved the thirst-ridden crops. Then Choni said that the rains had fallen enough and should go away. As he prayed, so they did.

Though Choni had rescued the people, the head priest sent for him and reproached the rainmaker for forcing God's hand. "Were you not Choni," said the priest, "I would pronounce a ban on you. But what can I do? You misbehave toward God and yet He does what you want… And about you the verse says, 'Your father and your mother should be glad and your mother should rejoice.' "

In common usage
Martainn MacGille Mhartainn, an eighteenth-century Scottish Gaelic writer,

is a taboo word in Hungary, for instance, even for those who can say the sneezy name. It refers to the Fair Lady, a beautiful demon with long hair who wears a gown as white as her heart is black. In colloquial usage, a sick child is sometimes said to be "suckled by the Fair Lady." She comes out during storms and hail to dance and seduce young men. Water dripping from eaves into a circular puddle constitutes a "platter," the space from which Fair Lady casts a spell — most potent at noon. Villagers are careful to evade such puddles or even a circle of short grass, since they may be the rings where Fair Lady dances out her malignant intentions.

In Russia and Poland old stories prevail about Nocritsa the Night Hag, also known as Kriksy and Plaksy. She torments children at night and in some regions mothers take precautions to keep the demon at bay. They draw a circle around a cradle with a knife, a double protection as it is believed that evil spirits cannot touch iron. Sometimes the knife is reinforced by an ax placed under the crib or cradle.

provides an excellent account of how circles had become customary to serve in everyday life:

"Some of the poorer sort of people in the Western Isles retain the custom of performing these circles sunwise about the persons of their benefactors three times, when they bless them, and wish good success to all their enterprises. Some are very careful when they set out to sea, that the boat be first rowed sunwise, and if this be neglected, they are afraid their voyage may prove unfortunate. I had this ceremony paid me when in Islay by a poor woman, after I had given her an alms. I desired her to let alone that compliment, for that I did not care for it; but she insisted to make these three ordinary turns, and then prayed that God and MacCharmaig, the patron saint of the island, might bless and prosper me in all my affairs.

"When a Gael goes to drink out of a consecrated fountain, he approaches it by going round the place from east to west, and at funerals, the procession observes the same direction in drawing near the grave. Hence also is derived the old custom of describing sunwise a circle, with a burning brand, about houses, cattle, corn and corn fields, to prevent their being burnt or in any way injured by evil spirits, or by witchcraft. The fiery circle was also made around women, as soon as possible after parturition, and also around newly born babes. These circles were, in later times, described by midwives, and were described effectual against the intrusion of *daoine sìth* or *sìthichean*, who were particularly on the alert in times of childhood, and not infrequently carried infants away, according to vulgar legends, and restored them afterwards, but sadly altered in features and personal appearance. Infants stolen by fairies are said to have voracious appetites, constantly craving for food. In this case it was usual for those who believed their children had been taken away, to dig a grave in the fields on quarter day and there to lay the fairy skeleton till next morning, at which time the parents went to the place, where they doubted not to find their own child in place of the skeleton."

– BARBARA STACY

The fascinating process for casting the ancient Lughnasadh Circle Ceremony is available on our website, at www.thewitchesalmanac.com.

77

Emma Hardinge Britten

Spiritualist medium, occultist — and witch!

ONE OF THE MOST interesting Spiritualists and occultists in the nineteenth century was Emma Hardinge Britten (1823-1899). Like many children born to impoverished families, Emma had to earn a living from a very young age. By the time she was twelve years old, she was working as a music teacher, a musician and an actress. During those years, she was also employed as a child clairvoyant by a secret society of male and female occultists that she called the Orphic Circle or Orphic Brotherhood (which she says was not its real name). This was in England.

To go by Emma's later account, the Orphic Circle met in its own lodge room, locked and guarded against intrusion, under a presiding Grand Master. Four child clairvoyants were stationed at the four points of the compass and each was provided with consecrated mirrors and crystals. These children were thrown into a trance by members of the society, who applied "currents of animal magnetism" to them. Incense, music and ritual aided their entrancement. The entranced children would travel on the astral plane to carry messages between the Orphic Circle and similar societies in other lands. Through them, too, the Circle would receive messages from spirits of various classes (generally not the spirits of the dead). Further, the Circle called other spirits into specially prepared mirrors and crystals that had been placed before the clairvoyant children. The members of the Orphic Circle were not traditional Christians: they did not believe in the immortality of the human soul or the resurrection of the dead.

Eventually Emma became too old to serve the Circle as a clairvoyant. She continued to work as an actress, and took on additional work as a reporter for theater journals. Later, in 1855, she left London for New York in hopes of building a theatrical career there. But that hope proved vain.

Strange are the ways of chance or fate! In New York, Emma encountered for the first time the brand-new religious movement known as Spiritualism. She found that her past service as a clairvoyant for the Orphic Circle had prepared her very well for the work of a Spiritualist medium—that is, an entranced person through whom the spirits of the dead communicated with the living at a séance. Emma had discovered a more lucrative career, and she threw herself into it with all the considerable talent and enthusiasm she could muster.

In the 1850s and 1860s, a séance would usually be held with only a few people present. One respected writer, Andrew Jackson Davis, thought that just twelve people, six men and six women, plus the medium, should be present at a séance. These thirteen people should sit in a circle and join hands, thereby amplifying an occult energy raised from their bodies, which was used to bring the spirits through to the sitters. (This energy was thought to resemble electricity or magnetism, and the circle of sitters was thought to store it up for the medium's use somewhat like electricity could be stored in a Leyden jar or a battery.)

While working as a medium in New York, Emma happened to meet an old friend on a visit from England, an occultist whom she had known from the Orphic Circle. They continued to exchange letters after his return to England. Under his influence, Emma's views on religion and occultism gradually changed. She had been a traditional Christian as a girl, and had been somewhat scandalized by the Orphic Circle's untraditional views. From 1860 onward, in all her public trance lectures and books, she became ever more critical of Christianity. In 1876 she went so far as to declare, in a leading Spiritualist newspaper (*The Banner of Light*), "Not being myself a professed Christian, I owe no allegiance to Christian dogmas."

At the same time, Emma also came out of the closet as an experienced occultist. In 1865, she began to give public lectures on subjects like "Modern Spiritualism and Witchcraft or Necromancy" and "Ancient Magic and Modern Spiritualism," in which she posited an occult power inherent in the human organism that was used alike by mediums now, and in ages past by magicians, necromancers and witches. There is no real difference, Emma said, between any of them: a medium is a magician is a necromancer is a witch. To be sure, some people were exceptionally gifted by nature in this respect, but almost anyone could become a medium or a magician or a necromancer or a witch with proper training — training that Emma hoped would become more freely available.

In 1875, Emma was one of a half dozen or so people who founded the Theosophical Society in New York. (Its first two meetings were held in her apartment.) A year later she published two remarkable books on occultism and magic, written under the influence of her old friend from the Orphic Circle, whom she identifies only as Chevalier Louis de B—.

The first of these books was titled *Art Magic*. It was a systematic treatise on magical theory and practice, and on the various orders of spirits with which magicians worked. It drew on many sources, some as old as the 1500s, but others by her own contemporaries, including unpublished writings by Frederick Hockley. So influential a witch as Doreen Valiente knew of *Art Magic* and praised it as a "very rare and remarkable old book" (in *The ABC of Witchcraft*, pp. 115-117.)

The second book was titled *Ghost Land*. It gave a fictionalized account of the Orphic Circle and Chevalier Louis's life in connection with it. In this guise it also develops the theory of working with spirits further than did *Art Magic*.

In light of all this, it is not surprising that here and there in her writings, Emma seems to embrace her identity as a witch-woman with a measure of veiled pride — though never quite so clearly as to give a Christian adversary a good opening to attack her. "I was 'born a witch,' as some of my public opponents have informed the world," she writes at the beginning of her *Autobiography*, published just after her death.

Emma is one of the earliest women to claim the identity of a witch in modern times, but she is not the only such woman: I have traced several others. Some were outspoken early feminists, occultists, or Spiritualists; others were just women living unconventional lives in obscurity. No doubt, too, some of these women passed their identity as witches down to their own daughters and granddaughters. There is an entire century of unknown Pagan witches here, roughly 1850-1950, just waiting for the spadework of scholars who are not afraid to break new ground.

– ROBERT MATHIESEN

Window on the Weather

The link between changing sunspots frequency and intensity is becoming more apparent during the current decade as the planet's temperature is impacted in ways consistent with previous historical periods. Similar to the early 1800s and 1700s, a tendency for cold winters to be focused in the Eastern half of the United States and Europe is evident. Similarly, the West Coast drought can be linked to this pattern; one that will ease some for a year or so with some implications for the growing season in those places. At mid-continent in the United States, abundant crops can be expected, in general for the next decade or so with below normal temperatures during the winter, followed by cool and damp summers — ideal weather for farmers. However, despite some drought relief in the short term, West Coast conditions can remain restrictive for some time. In particular, rainfall during the summer and fall will remain sparse, straining resources that do exist. Concurrent with the sunspot cycle present, Pacific ocean water temperatures are cooling, limiting available moisture for rainfall. This pattern will persist for some time and will spread dry conditions farther east into the southern United States. During this period, hurricane activity in both the Pacific and Atlantic Oceans is likely to remain subdued.

– Tom C. Lang

SPRING

MARCH 2016. Welcome drought relief arrives on the West Coast late this season and persists well into the Spring. The waning El Niño provides available moisture for rainfall and mountain snow, bringing relief to farmers available water supplies generally. Rainfall will be especially heavy from Los Angeles to the Bay area and will extend as far east as Phoenix as storms progress inland. Snow fall will end abruptly farther East after a rough winter, though the cold will linger, especially in the Northeast and Ohio Valley. Farther west and in the South snowfall will surprise residents in Dallas, Oklahoma and Kansas City after a mild early winter. While much of the country will experience below normal temperatures, Florida remains hot and dry with daily temperatures above 90 degrees much of the time. The first tornadoes of the season threaten Georgia.

APRIL 2016. Rainfall persists on the West Coast as the growing season begins there, an area stricken recently by severe drought. The snowpack in the Sierra Nevada remains deep, promising abundant water for some reservoirs in the months to come. Father east, a short and intense tornado season begins with the Mississippi Valley and southern Great Plains — the focus of the greatest frequency and intensity for severe weather. Mid to late afternoon is the time to be most alert there, though such storms can occur at any time. Spring's arrival is slowed by a lingering chill in the Northeast, with early flowers 10 to 14 days behind schedule. The mid Atlantic States are drenched by above normal rainfall, while the Southeast enjoys unseasonably warm weather by the 15th.

MAY 2016. The chance for a late season frost remains for inland valleys of the Northeast and Northwest while the rest of the nation enjoys a steady pace of climbing temperatures. Rainfall is abundant across the nations midsection with warm days and mild nights. Severe weather is occasional and generally limited to the Ohio Valley and Central Great Plains. The Central Valley in California enjoys a spell of crop recovery from recent rains. In the South, a preview of summer arrives with soaring temperatures, most noticeable in Florida and Texas. The mid Atlantic remains wet with frequent rainfall. Local flooding can be expected in hilly areas west of Washington, Baltimore and Philadelphia. A late season Nor'easter brings a wind-swept rain-soaked day to New England around the 20th.

SUMMER

JUNE 2016. Summer arrives with the promise of sunny days filled with warmth and pleasantly cool nights for mist. In the deep South, the humidity approaches oppressive levels by the 20th and thunderstorms are scattered in the afternoon. Florida's Gulf Coast experiences especially strong afternoon downpours. Several passing cold fronts brings gusty thunderstorms with hail a concern in a few. One or two tornadoes may be reported in New England and Eastern New York. Massachusetts and Connecticut are vulnerable this year. California and the entire West Coast return to dry conditions with an early season hurricane forming off the Baja. The central part of the country enjoys a beautiful stretch of weather, though some isolated severe conditions brought by late day thunderstorms is likely from the Dakotas into Minnesota.

JULY 2016. Haze, heat and humidity are present for much of the East Coast this month with temperatures soaring to the 90s from Florida to New England. Afternoon showers and thunderstorms are frequent, especially in hilly terrain where local flooding is possible. More stable conditions are likely near the coast where dense morning fog is slow to yield.

Farther west, cool air spreads pleasant weather across the Great Lake states and Great Plains as the growing season advances producing a bumper crop. Thunderstorms are a daily event, though scattered in Oklahoma and Texas. A monsoonal airflow from the eastern Pacific brings afternoon rain to the Continental divide from New Mexico to Western Montana. In California, winds can be strong in the Los Angles basin from the East, increasing the risk of brush fires.

AUGUST 2016. The hurricane season arrives with a slightly higher risk for a land falling storm compared to recent years. Western Atlantic development can be sudden. Early in this cycle, the entire Gulf Coast including Florida is at risk. All weather systems are slow moving during the month with heat remaining stagnant through much of the East. Conversely, pleasant weather remains the dominant theme from Indiana through the Great Plains. Thunderstorms forming from Atlanta to Charlotte and through the southern Appalachians are slow moving and can bring prolific rainfall over several hours. Ocean

swells are prominent along southern California beaches as offshore hurricanes form and pass well south. Strong daily thunderstorms can be expected along Florida's West Coast.

AUTUMN

SEPTEMBER 2016. The hurricane season reaches its peak in September with above normal activity this year. Florida to New England remains on alert from the risk of a land falling storm. All families there should have an emergency plan should an elevated alert become apparent. Cool weather arrives across the Rockies and Northern Plains with some record low temperatures possible there. Much of the country remains dry with the heaviest rainfall confined to the East Coast. The harvest arrives in the Midwest and Plains accompanied by sunny days. Temperatures are cooler than normal with the chance of a brief early season frost in Minnesota by the 30th. Much of the West Coast is tinder dry, as Pacific moisture remains lacking. Brush fires remain a concern at vulnerable locations. Steamy weather persists along the Gulf Coast.

OCTOBER 2016. Cool weather spreads south early this year across the Northern Rockies and the West Coast as far south as San Francisco. Passing showers bring Pacific air to Spokane and Boise with the highest mountains dusted by snow around the 20th. The harvest ends abruptly in the Dakotas as sub-freezing mornings arrive late in the month. Sunny and seasonable weather brings delightful climes to much of the East with fall colors arriving on time and brilliant this year from abundant rainfall. After an active season hurricanes diminish rapidly in the Atlantic and Pacific though the risk of a late season storm remains along the Gulf Coast. Winds remain gusty at times in Southern California. Denver can experience an early season snowfall by Halloween.

NOVEMBER 2016. Pleasantly cool fall weather signals a quiet approach to winter through much of the East. Normal rainfall and generally quiet weather can be expected there. Farther west, an early start to the cold season begins through the Plains and Rocky Mountain states, with a great variance in temperature as the days pass. Snows arrive with suddenness bringing a dusting to such cities as Denver and Boise. Snowfall also arrives in California's Sierra Nevada with lower elevation rainfall bringing welcome drought relief for many on the West Coast. Cooler weather overspreads the Gulf Coast and Florida by the 10th arriving with only brief showers.

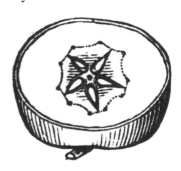

WINTER

DECEMBER 2016. Cold weather becomes well established from the Great Basin, Rocky Mountains and far West. Rainfall becomes more frequent as well, bringing water supplies to more acceptable levels. Farther east, a break in the recent string of severe winters can be expected with relatively mild weather for most locations east of Chicago. Mild temperatures will be accompanied by several wind-swept rainstorms that will soak a swath from Atlanta through the Ohio Valley, with balmy rains also arriving from Washington to Boston. A late season severe weather outbreak brings a flurry of tornadoes to Georgia and Central Florida. Texas and Oklahoma enjoy generally sunny and mild weather. Little snowfall is likely for much of the East this month.

JANUARY 2017. A welcome break from severe winter weather is likely in the East this year with the coldest and snowiest weather confined to areas west of the Mississippi River. This can have profound effects on the economy with lower energy costs and less disruption in industries dependent on efficient travel and outside working conditions. Snow will be generally light with a tendency for storms to begin as snow and then change to rain. In fact, many storms should be fast moving, not lasting more than about twelve hours. Cold and snowy weather will occur farther west with a fine ski season likely for Colorado, Utah and California's Sierra Nevada. With winter's most severe cold settling into the Great Basin and along the Continental Divide, the impact of winter weather will affect less populated areas than in recent years, giving the nation a welcome break from its effects.

FEBRUARY 2017. Several weeks of snowy weather can be expected in parts of the East, though snowfall should average below normal. Days should be relatively mild, reaching the 40s in New England and Ohio Valley. Below zero days will occur only on few days early in the month there while the Southeast enjoys an early taste of Spring reaching the 70s regularly after the 20th from Georgia through Florida. Ice on the Great Lakes is less extensive than in recent years making shipments through the Port of Chicago easier. Snow and cold persists in the West with far above normal snowfall in mountainous regions from California to Colorado. Phoenix enjoys some brief but memorable winter rainfall with desert flowers in full bloom. Denver is impacted by heavy snowfall twice during the month with excellent skiing at nearby ski areas. The Great Plains are snow free and seasonably cold much of the time.

⋛ Hazel ⋚

Coll

NINE IS A MAGIC NUMBER and the ninth consonant of the Druid's alphabet belongs to the tree of wisdom, poetic art and divination — the magical hazel tree.

Unprepossessing to look at, more a spreading bush than a tree, the hazel rarely exceeds 12 feet in height. Bright brown bark mottled with grey, male and female catkins hanging like tassels, and oval leaves with toothed edges are identifying marks of the hazel. Hazel thickets provide winter cover for wildlife. Its branches in time past served as fences, pea poles, clothes props and secured thatch for roofs of cottages. Excellent kindling wood, the hazel was the first choice of bakers for their ovens.

The magical significance of hazel crosses cultural lines, for it appears in the lore of Northern and Southern Europe and the Near East. The staff of the Roman god Mercury was of hazel wood. The myths say Apollo presented the caduceus to Hermes, the Greek counterpart of Mercury, in recognition of his mystical power to calm human passion and improve virtue. The medieval magician's wand was traditionally cut from the hazel tree with scrupulous ceremony drawn from Hebraic sources. Ancient Irish heralds carried white hazel wands. The "wishing rods" of Teutonic legend were cut from the hazel tree.

Hazel's function as a divining tool is many centuries old. The forked hazel-stick employed by dowsers to discover underground water sources, mineral deposits and buried treasure is still in use today as it was before the turn of the Christian era.

Hazelnuts, often called filberts, are used as charms to promote fertility. Charles Godfrey Leland says "a rosary of hazelnuts brings good luck when hung in a house, and hazelnut necklaces found in prehistoric tombs were probably amulets as well as ornaments." Hazelnuts turn up in a variety of forms of love divination: share a double nut with someone you love and if silence is maintained while the nuts are eaten, your love will grow.

QUADRUPLE OR NOTHING

An introduction to Hermetic number theory

Much human ingenuity has gone into finding the ultimate Before. The current state of knowledge can be summarized thus: In the beginning, there was nothing, which exploded.

    – Terry Pratchett, *Lords and Ladies*

FOR AS LONG AS we have record, humanity has placed a rather special emphasis upon numbers in one way or another: Four Horsemen, Twelve Apostles, Seven Gates of Thebes and so forth. Occultists are no different in this regard.

Now, a large portion of Hermetic theory comes from ancient philosophers like Pythagoras, Parmenides and Plato. Plato's *Timaeus* was particularly important in establishing a cosmology centered around the sanctity of numbers, elements, geometric forms and divine emanations. His later admirers, such as Plotinus, Porphyry and Iamblichus, took things even further.

To get a really good grasp of how numbers became viewed as mystical things, let's start at the beginning, and I mean the very beginning, with Nothing. At least, we'll call it Nothing. Ultimately, we're talking about the state of the universe before creation, before the Big Bang; before anything that could even be called a Something came about. We call it Nothing for convenience, but frankly, our minds have a lot of trouble with Nothing, since even our conception of Nothing is still Something. Eventually, however, Nothing indeed became Something.

•

One. The first inkling of creation. That miniature speck. That ultimate unity. The Monad. The seed of the entire universe, contained within a pinprick. However, our Monad could not remain as merely One. It might as well revert back to being Nothing, since an ultimate unity containing everything would still lack distinction from anything else. Therefore, our One had to notice that it was something other than the something from which it came. The Monad awakened then, and became self-reflective.

••

A Dyad was thus generated. Though the initial Monad was perfect in every way, it could not create an exact replica of itself. Number Two just had to be a different kettle of creation, even if only slightly, else it would merely be a case of the One interacting with itself. Instead, One became Two. Or, geometrically speaking, the Point became the Line.

———

Conveniently, the moment the Dyad was created, everything else in the Universe pretty much followed suit almost immediately. Allow me to elaborate. The moment something has Two points, it instantly also has a Third, since there must automatically be a mean, or halfway-point between the Two, that may act as a perfect point of balance. When that balance point expands, something magical happens.

Behold, the Triad. Ever wonder why the "Third time's a charm?" Or why doing something three times "makes it stick," so to speak? "Trinities?" "Triple Goddesses?" "Thrice Greatest?" They all come back to our pal, the triangle. The ancient philosophers believed that all creation was dependent upon sacred geometric properties. The Triangle is the first and simplest of all polygons and is used to create all of the others. Two Triangles make a Square, Three make a Pentagon, and so forth. Thus, the number Three became synonymous with manifestation. For One became Two, Two became Three, and Three became the cornerstone of creation. In addition, each triangle thus created could be split a theoretically infinite number of times, creating a theoretically infinite number of triangles.

However, our ancient philosophers knew that a flat world was a boring world indeed. Our two-dimensional polygon of three sides needed some depth. Enter the Tetrad.

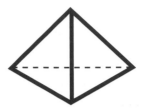

Number Four. The sacred. The holy. Now in glorious 3D! Why was Four such a big deal? Because not only did it represent the culmination of the "divine mind," finally achieving a 3-dimensional state (thus becoming a true building block of our gloriously lumpy universe), but because the sacred Ten — the number (usually) of the first digits we ever used to count with, which all of the other numbers greater than Ten are based upon — is found within the Tetrad. You see, when the number Four unfolds, it becomes the Tetractys.

1 plus 2 plus 3 plus 4 equals 10. The pattern, in perfect symmetry, folds out into the first polygon, the cornerstone of creation, made from the numerical key of the cosmos, i.e. the digits from one to ten contained within the Tetractys, or one through four, symbolic of physical creation from point to line to plane to

solid. Also, we cannot forget to mention the 4 elements intrinsic to creation: Fire, Water, Air and Earth.

The Four that is Three may also partially be why the number 7 is deemed sacred, though there's also a bunch of correspondences to the Seven Holy Planets, Seven Stars of the Pleiades, and so forth.

But to really see how these concepts were encapsulated, we must bring alphabets into the mix.

Greek	Hebrew	Number
Alpha A α	Aleph א	1
Beta B β	Beth ב	2
Gamma Γ γ	Gimel ג	3
Delta Δ δ	Daleth ד	4

Many of the ancient texts revered by Hermeticists were written in derivations of either ancient Greek or Hebrew, and both cultures had based their alphabets upon the earlier Phoenician letters. Initially, none of these cultures had a numerical system separate from their alphabet, so they used letters to represent their numbers.

Thus 1, 2, 3, 4 became Aleph, Beth, Gimel and Daleth for the Hebrews and Alpha, Beta, Gamma, and Delta for the Greeks. You'll note that number 4 for the Greeks (and the Phoenicians) was represented by the Triangle, which symbolized both the 1 becoming 3 and the 4 becoming 10 (when viewed as the Tetractys). Simultaneously, the Greek word for Ten of something, or Deka (δεκα), starts with the letter Delta. Still with me? Now comes the best part.

The Letter used to represent Ten of something was this:

Iota. Ever hear someone say "I don't give one iota..." of something? This is where that phrase comes from. Iota is not only tiny, but also the proverbial mustard seed of the entire Greek alphabet (and subsequent language), since every other letter was first written using a series of Iotas. This is even more visually striking when you play with the Hebrew Iota, known as Yod.

An initial spark. A tiny candle flame. The first smudge of a paintbrush or calligraphy pen. The beginning of creation.

Much like One eventually became Ten, our Ten can now become One again. Dekad becomes Monad and the circle is complete.

So, to recap: Nothing became 1, 1 became 2, 2 became 3, 3 became 4, 4 became 10, 10 represented everything in the Universe, and condensed back to One, which might as well be Nothing!

– ANTHONY TETH

89

Magic that Works

FROM A PAGAN perspective, the visible world is the expression of a reality that both permeates and transcends it. From this it follows that behind its rich diversity lies a subtle unity, which, in turn, reflects the inter-connectedness of its myriad parts. As Hinduism puts it, these are but the million faces of Brahman. Herein lies the secret why magic — real magic, that is, not the smoke and mirrors kind — actually works.

For centuries, the words "magic" and "witchcraft" have been virtually interchangeable, although surviving records make it hard to distinguish between what witches got up to in the past and what their accusers invented or, for that matter, what witches themselves invented in order to satisfy their tormentors. Interestingly enough, among the lurid tales of orgies, curses, familiars and demons, well captured by Goya

Chick with infant head,
from *Los Caprichos,* by Goya.

in his paintings, there is mention also of nocturnal feasts, allegedly presided over by a goddess, where the serious business of magic was conducted. This last detail is sometimes overlooked by those who argue, not completely without justification, that modern witchcraft is the invention of an ex-colonial civil servant on the south coast of England close to seventy years ago. It is indisputable that without a touch of magic, there is no such thing as witchcraft.

The art of causing change

What has by now become a standard definition of magic was provided by Aleister Crowley, no saint, but no monster either, who defined it as "the art of causing change to occur in conformity with the will." Dion Fortune, his more respectable contemporary, called it "the art of causing changes to occur in consciousness" but this tells us little, as changes in consciousness can be induced by a variety of means, among them drugs, meditation and fasting, none of which requires us to put on ceremonial dress or, as the case may be, strip off and invoke Pagan gods. No, by 'change,' Crowley certainly meant more than a different state of awareness from our everyday one.

To understand the mechanics of magic, so to speak, we have to remind ourselves that reality is more, far more, than what our senses reveal. It is presumptuous to think otherwise, implying, as it does, that nothing can exist

unless it is perceptible. Even scientists believe otherwise, now that particle physics have demonstrated that the smallest components of matter straddle a frontier between the spatial-temporal world we occupy and another, no less real, in which neither space nor time exists. Not only is the latter beyond our understanding but also beyond our conceptual reach, given that our imagination is nourished by our environment and nothing outside it.

The miracle of the One thing

Only by analogy can we attempt to grasp what lies beyond, since, although both are manifestly different, the "here" that is familiar to us and the inconceivable "there" are essentially one and the same. It is this unity and the relationships among its myriad parts that magic seeks to exploit. In words attributed to the legendary Hermes Trismegistus "that which is above is like that which is below, to accomplish the miracle of the One thing."

The same principle applies as much to the world around, as to any hypothetical reality beyond it. It permits us to adopt what I call an "integrated" approach to the natural world, one that enables us to discern the implicit unity among its many parts. Thanks to this and, as Dion Fortune would maintain, to an appropriate change in consciousness, we are able, for example, to discern the hidden virtues of plants,

whether medical or magical, something witches have traditionally been doing for centuries. It explains why the local cunning man or woman is still esteemed in rural Wales where I grew up.

Eye of the soul

What he or she does, of course, is discern the very being of things, thereby observing the landscape with what Jakob Boehme, the Silesian mystic, famously called the "eye of the soul."

The technique can be mastered by anyone minded to do so. Yet, like many traditional practices, it is often overlooked by contemporary witches, either because most live in towns or cities and have lost touch with the countryside, even with Nature herself, or because they prefer working with fellow coven members at what they regard as more exciting stuff. For many, ritual and the company of others are preferable to a solitary walk in the woods. More's the pity.

But then the preference is understandable. Few would deny, after all, that magic is most vividly experienced in a semi-formal setting where it emerges from the collaborative effort of several people, all compatible and all prepared to work together more or less harmoniously. (I say "more or less" because a little rivalry, even a hint of tension, can sometimes add zest to the proceedings.) It then becomes far easier to gain access to supra-sensible reality, a condition — for we can hardly call it a "place" — that goes by a variety of names, one of the most popular being the Inner Planes.

Correspondences sympathetic and symptomatic

We reach this supra-sensible reality by attaining a higher level of consciousness, helped by the impact of symbols, colours, sounds and scents, as well as the overall "choreography" of the ritual proceedings. These elements will have been selected with an eye on the aim of the operation and on whatever supernatural being or force is to be evoked. Here, use is made of the "correspondences" sympathetic to it and, if you like, symptomatic of it. With their assistance, we aspire to exchange the conditioned reality we normally occupy for the unconditioned one beyond it and thereby "earth" so to speak, a specific impulse within it.

As the 19th century magus, Eliphas Lévi declared, "Analogy" — represented by the "correspondences" we've assembled — "is the last word of science and the first word of faith... the sole possible mediator between the visible and the invisible, between the finite and the infinite."

But magic is nothing if not practical and, as such, it has a purpose beyond passive enjoyment of a heightened awareness, always at risk of degenerating into mere self-indulgence.

Outward vesture

Lévi, whose given name at birth was Alphonse-Louis Constant, described ritual as the "outward vesture" of every magical operation, by which he meant that its function was to serve and stimulate the volitional and creative powers of the imagination, so that a specific objective might be attained. Experience does indeed show that the more involved participants become in what happens around them — seduced, as it were, by the "outward vesture" — the greater the energy available to realize a collective intention. In addition, should conditions be right, it may even contrive to render objective whatever is visualized, a process familiar to psychical researchers and known in the East as *kriyashakti*. It enables archetypal forms and other entities not of this world to take on form and substance in our midst, seemingly every bit as solid as ourselves.

A quasi-sacramental quality

It would nevertheless be wrong to think of Lévi's "outward vesture" as no more than a means to this end and devoid of any merit of its own. The truth is that through long association the elements which comprise it become imbued with the very forces they purport to represent, acquiring in the process a quasi-sacramental quality. (A sacrament is defined by theologians as the visible sign of an invisible grace.) Thus, a given symbol not only points to a supernatural reality, itself inexpressible, but, more importantly, contains something of its essence. That is why meticulous attention must be paid to getting the details of a magical operation exactly right. Failure to do so may not lead to catastrophe, although some people have come perilously close, but it does mean that one's magical efforts will have been in vain.

On the other hand, if one goes by the book, then success is guaranteed. Again this is due to the sacramental quality of the outward vesture, for success proceeds from the ritual itself and not from the merits of whoever performs it, a consequence theologians sum up rather well by distinguishing between the act (*ex opere operatis*) and the agent responsible for its execution (*ex opere operantis*). Certainly the lesson for ceremonial magicians and witches alike is to get the details right each and every time.

The educated will

All of which may seem far removed from the spells and good luck charms — let's not mention the curses — for which old-fashioned witches were long famed. In all cases, however, the principle remains the same, for as Lévi points out, "a practice, even though it be superstitious and foolish, will be efficacious because it is a realization of the will." Elsewhere he refers to it as the "educated" will and on this Aleister Crowley would later base his personal philosophy, opting to call it, with a brief nod to Rabelais, the Law of Thelema. (Crowley, born eight months after Lévi's death in 1875, declared himself to be none other than an incarnation of that magus.)

It makes sense, for, all things considered, it is indeed our will that ultimately sponsors the changes magic brings about, whether these occur inside our consciousness, as Dion Fortune maintained, or objectively in the world around us. Given the Hermetic connection between the microcosm that is each of us and the macrocosm that is everything, we are entitled to regard every informed act of will as a local manifestation of that supreme will which quickens and directs the universe itself.

Yes indeed, magic works.

– DAVID CONWAY

93

THE SPINSTER

A RATHER well-to-do textile merchant, having earned both a sizable fortune and blusterous reputation, was fond of proclaiming (loudly and to anyone who would listen) all the various ways in which his life had turned out better than most. In the tavern, the town square or the market; to the butcher, baker or blacksmith – the merchant took every opportunity to let it be known that his wares were the finest, his wife the most beautiful and his daughter the most talented. Most folk familiar with the man's penchant for verbose declarations understood them to be harmless hyperbole, so when the merchant said, "My daughter is such an uncommonly gifted spinner she could spin flax into gold!", most within earshot understood he was speaking metaphorically.

Unfortunately, one who stood within earshot was a very literally minded prince. This prince also happened to come from a very flax rich and gold poor country, so he was naturally intrigued by the prospect of a woman who could solve this imbalance.

"If your daughter is as talented as you say, she should have no trouble turning my flax surplus into a vast treasure pile! If she can spin one hectare of flax into any amount of gold in three days, I will make her my princess! But, if she fails... well, vexed princes can be rather creative when it comes to punishment." Before the merchant could even attempt a basic explanation of the concept of analogy, the deal was done and the prince was gone, vowed to return in three days time to either collect his gold and his bride or else dole out some capriciously conceived retribution.

To the merchant's surprise, his daughter was not at all worried by the news of his blunder. "Have the flax delivered to the spinsters on the edge of town. I will take care of the rest." And so the flax and the daughter disappeared over the horizon, leaving the merchant alone with his thoughts.

For three days the merchant waited anxiously. He paced around his house in complete silence, consumed by the prospect of losing his business, his family, his mind – all because he couldn't keep his mouth shut! Just as the merchant was at his most despondent, his daughter returned, carrying a rather generous satchel of gold. The

prince arrived shortly after, and upon seeing the exquisite beauty of the merchant's daughter, nearly forgot about the promised gold. When the golden bounty was revealed the prince enthusiastically declared the royal wedding should take place as soon as possible, for a woman of such rare looks and talent was deserving of royal status. And so the prince was off to make arrangements post haste.

"My darling!" cried the merchant, "how did you pull it off? How did you turn flax into gold?"

His daughter laughed. "Father, a gifted merchant such as yourself should know better. I simply did what you do every day! First, I had the spinsters sort and separate the flax. They spun the finer threads into linen while I sold the seeds to the spice traders and the course fibers to the rope makers. Then I sold the linen at a premium and well, here we are!"

"But my darling, the prince will expect you to literally spin flax into gold for the rest of your days! The jig will be up and you will be in danger!"

She smiled slyly. "Don't worry. I've taken care of that too."

The day of the wedding arrived with customary fanfare. The prince invited dignitaries from all adjacent kingdoms and the merchant invited all the leaders of the merchant community.

Amongst this illustrious crowd sat, rather conspicuously, three old women of unfortunate appearance. Their backs were hunched and twisted, their fingers swollen and arthritic. They were of such striking appearance that the prince could not help but notice them, so he asked his new bride:

"Sweetheart, who are those old crones? I know I didn't invite them…"

"Oh, those are the dear old spinsters who taught me everything I know! Poor things. They've been deformed from a lifetime of sitting behind the spinning wheel. Oh well! Such is the price to pay for talent such as ours."

The prince was at once horrified and forbid the newly minted princess to ever spin again. "Gold is well and good, but a beautiful woman is worth much more!"

The merchant overheard the exchange and gently chuckled to himself. The prince may value beauty over gold, but the merchant knew a keen mind like his daughters' was worth far more.

– a Grimm retelling by
SHANNON MARKS

MEXICO'S NIGHT OF THE RADISHES

Celebration of Yuletide, south of the border

EL NOCHE DE RABANOS, the Night of the Radishes, is among the most intriguing and unusual of the many annual celebrations and folk festivals which honor the winter solstice around the world. Celebrated only in Oaxaca, Mexico, this event is a unique kind of art show which attracts huge crowds. Enthusiastic visitors, both young and old, form lines that are miles long. Ironically, this gathering is almost unheard of in other parts of the world.

The Night of the Radishes was first celebrated in Oaxaca on December 23, 1897. The legend is that a local merchant hoped to attract customers to his shop in El Zocolo, the village plaza. He began to carve the white and ruby skin of radishes. Beautiful and festive displays emerged, as if by magic. The talented entrepreneur's cheerful radish carvings were instantly popular with shoppers, who purchased them for holiday table centerpieces. This part of Mexico has a long tradition of wood carving. Soon other farmers and vegetable peddlers joined in to try their hands at carving radishes to make decorations, too. The festival officially became an annual part of the Yuletide holiday when Oaxaca's mayor proclaimed December 23 as the Night of the Radishes.

For more than a century now, artists, professional artisans and amateurs alike, have gathered in Oaxaca. The competitive spirit intensifies yearly. The would-be artists eagerly try hard to out-do each other. The humble radish has been glorified and is now a star in its own right. Over time, special gigantic varieties of radishes have been developed. Not meant to be eaten, these super celebrities are large and heavy. They can weigh 5 lbs. or more and grow to be over a yard long. The city has dedicated special plots of land to farming radishes. Agricultural experts are employed to supervise their growth and distribute them among the 100 or more contestants near the winter solstice.

Starting around December 18, the artists collect the radishes they need and begin to carve. They must work quickly for the vegetables begin to curl and turn brown in a short time. Nativity scenes, dancers, flowers, musical instruments,

Mayan images, mission-style architecture and local wild life, including snakes and alligators, are popular themes. The carving stops on December 23 when the judging begins. A grand prize of 12,000 pesos is presented to the artist whose radish art is judged to be the best.

The 21st century finds the Night of the Radishes becoming bigger and brighter each year. In order to encourage the next generation of radish carvers, a special competition for young people aged 6 to 17 years of age has recently been inaugurated. Fireworks, floats and large holiday dinners are now a part of the celebrations in Oaxaca each December 23.

– ELAINE NEUMEIER

Dulce Regional Oaxaqueño by Carlos Laurencio Vazquez Sebastian at the 2014 Noche de Rabanos in the city of Oaxaca, Mexico, 24 December 2014.

POPE FRANCIS

The people's Pope

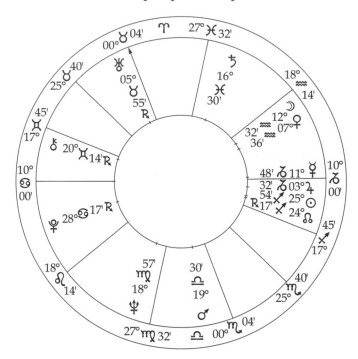

EACH YEAR *The Witches' Almanac* features a celebrity horoscope, exploring the birth chart of one who has impacted the magical universe. Our choice this year might be a surprise. Called the People's Pope, within weeks days of assuming the papacy Pope Francis became a global celebrity. With his charming simplicity, cheerful compassion and respectful acceptance of all kinds of people and lifestyles, Pope Francis has been called the most popular person on the planet by some. Perhaps the Sabian symbols listed in his horoscope will offer insights into his magic and charisma, now being called "The Francis Effect."

The Galactic Center is prominent in his birth chart. It conjoins his Sun and Moon's north node in the last decanate of Sagittarius. The energy is progressive and indicates expansion regarding his philosophy about faith, the law, academia, ethics and a vision of the future. He is also an enthusiastic football fan. The Sagittarius placements make an out-of-sign conjunction with Jupiter in Capricorn. This is a favorable aspect promising a zest for life and an expansive outlook. The Capricorn influence also suggests a practical application of theological ideals. All three placements are in his 6th house. This shows a perfectionist dedicated to conscientious service and a love of animals. St. Francis of Assisi, whose name he assumed upon accepting the papacy, is the beloved patron of animals and the poor.

That powerful 6th house influence also hints at his preference for simplicity and economy. Even after rising to the rank of cardinal, Francis chose to live in a plain apartment instead of the luxurious residence the Church would have provided. Pope Francis has the Moon and Venus conjunct in Aquarius in the 7th house. Humanitarian ideals, originality, attunement to the future, and charisma coupled with an ability to relate to all kinds of people are indicated. During the first year of his papacy, world leaders were excited to meet with him, as he became *Time Magazine's* Person of the Year. Uranus is in Taurus in the 10th house in mutual reception with Venus in Aquarius in the 7th house This is electrical, controversial, surprising and shows sudden changes of fame and fortune. On very controversial topics Francis' statements have had a tremendous impact.

Abortion, gay rights, women priests and the acceptance of divorce are previous taboos he has begun to relax. Pope Francis has Cancer rising. At a glance this is mild, humble and self effacing, but there is also Pluto in the 1st house bringing depth, intensity of purpose, and a transformative effect. His role seems pastoral and healing, but Pluto reveals that much stirs beneath the surface. He is astute, clever and an exceptionally good listener, employing the media, including Twitter, to get the message of his 1st century office across to the 21st century masses. Pope Francis seems to raise hope globally that a better world is emerging, winning the approval of Pagans, Protestants, Jews, Muslims, lapsed Catholics and agnostics alike.

– DIKKI-JO MULLEN

POPE FRANCIS

Jorge Mario Bergoglio was born December 17, 1936
at 9:00 pm ADT in Buenos Aires, Argentina

Data Table
Tropical Placidus Houses

SUN 25 Sagittarius 54, 6th house, 26th degree of Sagittarius
Sabian symbol: A flag-bearer in a battle — This degree overshadows individual ambitions to accent the supremacy of common ideals. Nobility and self sacrifice are suggested.

MOON 12 Aquarius 32, 7th house (waxing Moon in the crescent phase), 13th degree of Aquarius
Sabian symbol: A barometer — This shows an effective estimation of potentials. It indicates keen observation and exceptional competence in using good judgment.

MERCURY 11 Capricorn 48, 7th house, 12th degree of Capricorn
Sabian symbol: A student of nature lecturing — Self confidence through acquiring knowledge and a practical application of values are illustrated here.

VENUS 7 Aquarius 36, 7th house, 8th degree of Sagittarius
Sabian symbol: Beautifully gowned wax figures — Impact is a keynote here. A dramatization leads to reorganizing what is real within the human character.

MARS 19 Libra 30, 3rd house, 20th degree of Libra
Sabian symbol: A Jewish rabbi — Heritage and a social nature is stressed. Dedication to a group advances the aspirations for all.

JUPITER 3 Capricorn 32, 6th house, 4th degree of Capricorn
Sabian symbol: A party entering a large canoe — This shows an exceptional capacity for bringing together a group for effective accomplishment.

SATURN 16 Pisces 30, 8th house, 17th degree of Pisces
Sabian symbol: An Easter promenade — There is a mood of celebration, refinement and inspiration shown. Saturn represents responsibility, and the sign of Pisces has a special link with the Christian Church. It was Easter week of 2013 when Francis first assumed the most important papal duties.

URANUS 5 Taurus 55 (retrograde), 10th house, 6th degree of Taurus
Sabian symbol: A bridge being built across a gorge — Difficulties and physical limitations are surmounted by clever design and planning.

NEPTUNE 18 Virgo 57, 2nd house, 19th degree of Virgo
Sabian symbol: A swimming race — This illustrates the process of eliminating what is substandard or unacceptable. Neptune is always a spiritual influence, related to religion. Francis I has done much to eliminate the abuses within the Catholic Church. For example, he has abolished the horrible title of Monsignor, which encouraged negative power plays for advancement among ambitious priests.

PLUTO 28 Cancer 17 (retrograde), 1st house, 29th degree of Cancer
Sabian symbol: A Greek muse weighs in golden scales just-born twins — This emphasizes values. Good judgment through careful consideration is suggested.

CHIRON 20 Gemini 14 (retrograde), 12th house, 21st degree of Gemini
Sabian symbol: A labor demonstration — This message is one of courage and seeking effective representation.

NORTH NODE OF THE MOON (true node), 24 Sagittarius 16, 25th degree of Sagittarius
Sabian symbol: A chubby boy on a hobbyhorse — Determination despite setbacks and using the skills and tools available to the best advantage is the message.

PART OF FORTUNE 26 Leo 39, 2nd house, 27th degree of Leo
Sabian symbol: Daybreak — Recapturing the potentials of life through a new beginning; cycles of change and resurgence are shown. Cardinal Jorge Bergoglio was preparing to retire when a surprising turn of events led him to the Papacy. The Sabian symbol here is for the fortunate dawn, the daybreak of a whole new life.

ASCENDENT (rising sign) 10 Cancer 00, 11th degree of Cancer
Sabian Symbol: A clown making grimaces — This sharpens the impact one individual has on others. The everyday personality has memorable characteristics.

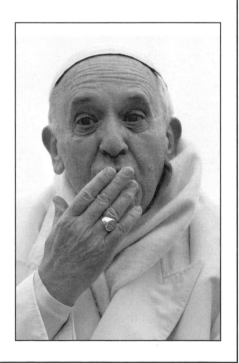

THE SABIAN SYMBOLS

THE EARLIEST documented astrological traditions are traced to the ancient civilizations of East Africa and Western Asia. Artifacts include the renowned sandstone bas relief zodiac from the Temple of Hathor at Dendera in Egypt. Its age is disputed, with some scholars dating it to the New Kingdom, while others place it in the Graeco-Roman era.

Modern Western astrology derives predominately from ancient Mesopotamia. The Magi of Persia were renowned stargazers, as was the patriarch Abraham, widely considered to be the progenitor of the "Abrahamic religions": Judaism, Christianity and Islam. Not least, astrology has potent associations with the mysterious land of Saba.

Marc Edmund Jones

Mysterious Saba

Controversy exists as to the historic location of Saba with some authorities placing it in Ethiopia, while others believe it to have been in Yemen. (Still others think that ancient Saba may have encompassed both regions.) Dr. Marc Edmund Jones (1888-1980), widely considered the "dean of American astrology," identified the Sabians as the fifth sub-race of the Atlantean root race and associated them with the inhabitants of ancient Sumer.

The mysterious history of Saba and its proximity to sacred and spiritual places appealed to Dr. Jones and inspired the name he chose for the system of astrology that he developed: the Sabian symbols. The 360 Sabian symbols are unique and separate images, each one depicting a degree of the zodiac.

Visionary experiences

Dr. Jones sought to have the Sabian symbols revealed through visionary experiences. His first attempts involved one of his students, artist and psychic, Zoe Wells. Her attempts at attunement and channeling the symbols did not wholly satisfy Jones, but she did provide an important point about the concept of individual zodiacal degree symbolism. It was Zoe Wells who first suggested that it originated in the astrological traditions of Arabia and Egypt.

Jones came across an obscure set of pictorial symbols for the degrees of the zodiac by Welsh astrologer Charubel (John Thomas), which were first published in Alan Leo's 1898 *Astrological Manual*. Although Jones felt the symbols were too dated and not sufficiently universal, he liked the concept of bringing each zodiacal degree to life using pictures.

During one single day in 1925 (the date wasn't recorded), Jones collaborated successfully with Elsie Wheeler, a gifted clairvoyant and another of his students, to complete the Sabian symbols project. Their work has had a profound impact on horoscope interpretation ever since.

One fell swoop

Jones and Wheeler were both in their late thirties. They had met about two years earlier when Wheeler joined Jones' Spiritualist church. So crippled with arthritis that she was confined to a wheelchair and could barely move her head or arms, Elsie nevertheless made an excellent living as a medium. She often lamented to Marc, her friend and minister, that she wanted to produce something profound and significant. Jones approached Elsie Wheeler with the thought that connecting with a higher intelligence to retrieve the zodiacal symbols just might be the project that would help her to realize this wish.

Jones was adamant that this had to be accomplished in "one fell swoop" without any interruptions. Having prepared 360 index cards listing each zodiacal degree, he collected Elsie, who had to be carried to his car. They then drove to an isolated area in San Diego's Balboa Park. A massive feat of channeling, connecting to the universal mind matrix for many hours, followed while the two sat in the parked car. Marc took notes and Elsie spoke in a trance. The symbols she described that day range from abstract to humorous to gruesome, absurd and mystical.

Profound insights

Marc Edmund Jones credits Dane Rudhyar, another great 20th century astrologer, with helping him to organize and popularize the Sabian symbols for publication in 1953. Originally, they were presented as mimeographed astrology lessons. Gradually, students began to remark upon the profound insights the images brought to analyzing natal horoscopes and in forecasting the future. The Sabian Assembly was established as a group dedicated to continue researching the symbols. The enigmatic images are revelations, which are thought to connect to the deeper meaning of individual birth charts and to horoscopes charting world events including weather and politics.

When using the Sabian symbols to interpret a horoscope, first consider the images for the ascendant, Sun, Moon and planets. Later the descendant, midheaven and nadir may be added for more detail. Jones taught that it is crucial to remember that the Sabian symbols are read forward. For example, Pope Francis was born with his sun at 25 degrees Sagittarius 54 minutes. Thus, the Sabian symbol for his sun will be 26 degrees Sagittarius.

– DIKKI-JO MULLEN

Get more information about Sabian Symbols when you visit our Almanacs Extra page at http://TheWitchesAlmanac.com/ AlmanacExtras/.

The Dumb Book

IN THE HIGH ROAD which led through a wood stood a solitary farmhouse; the road, in fact, ran right through its yard. The sun was shining and all the windows were open; within the house people were very busy. In the yard, in an arbour formed by lilac bushes in full bloom, stood an open coffin; thither they had carried a dead man, who was to be buried that very afternoon. Nobody shed a tear over him; his face was covered over with a white cloth, under his head they had placed a large thick book, the leaves of which consisted of folded sheets of blotting-paper, and withered flowers lay between them; it was the herbarium which he had gathered in various places and was to be buried with him, according to his own wish. Every one of the flowers in it was connected with some chapter of his life.

"Who is the dead man?" we asked.

"The old student," was the reply. "They say that he was once an energetic young man, that he studied the dead languages, and sang and even composed many songs; then something had happened to him, and in consequence of this he gave himself up to drink, body and mind. When at last he had ruined his health, they brought him into the country, where someone paid for his board and residence. He was gentle as a child as long as the sullen mood did not come over him; but when it came he was fierce, became as strong as a giant, and ran about in the wood like a chased deer. But when we succeeded in bringing him home, and prevailed upon him to open the book with the dried-up plants in it, he would sometimes sit for a whole day looking at this or that plant, while frequently the tears rolled over his cheeks. God knows what was in his mind; but he requested us to put the book into his coffin, and now he lies there. In a little while the lid will be placed upon the coffin, and he will have sweet rest in the grave!"

The cloth which covered his face was lifted up; the dead man's face expressed peace — a sunbeam fell upon it. A swallow flew with the swiftness of an arrow into the arbour, turning in its flight, and twittered over the dead man's head.

What a strange feeling it is — surely we all know it —to look through old letters of our young days; a different life rises up out of the past, as it were, with all its hopes and sorrows. How many of the people with whom in those days we used to be on intimate terms appear to us as if dead, and yet they are still alive — only we have not thought of them for such a long time, whom we imagined we should retain in our memories for ever, and share every joy and sorrow with them.

The withered oak leaf in the book here recalled the friend, the schoolfellow, who was to be his friend for life. He fixed the leaf to the student's cap in the green wood, when they vowed eternal friendship. Where does he dwell now? The leaf is kept, but the friendship does no longer exist. Here is a foreign hothouse plant, too tender for the gardens of the North. It is almost as if its leaves still smelt sweet! She gave it to him out of her own garden — a nobleman's daughter.

Here is a water-lily that he had plucked himself, and watered with salt tears – a lily of sweet water. And here is a nettle: what may its leaves tell us? What might he have thought when he plucked and kept it? Here is a little snowdrop out of the solitary wood;

here is an evergreen from the flower-pot at the tavern; and here is a simple blade of grass.

The lilac bends its fresh fragrant flowers over the dead man's head; the swallow passes again — twit, twit;" now the men come with hammer and nails, the lid is placed over the dead man, while his head rests on the dumb book — so long cherished, now closed for ever!

– Hans Christian Andersen

A Talisman for Love, Trust and Conquest

KEYS HAVE BEEN intertwined with the human experience since the dawn of civilization. They seem to have first appeared in ancient Egypt at least 4000 years ago. The earliest keys were created from a complex series of knotted hand-woven ropes. Some were very heavy and fashioned from wood. Then, about 1500 years ago, the modern key began to evolve with increasingly elaborate mechanisms. At first, upon considering keys, they can be dismissed as mere mundane and practical tools, useful for simply granting easy access or assuring protection. Eventually, along the way, like the treasures and secrets they might guard, they began to develop a powerful mystique. Over the centuries keys have become cher-

ished as potent talismans. In addition to assuring physical security and control, keys began to be linked to a myriad of deeper magical functions and symbolisms. Since the 19th Century keys have become very beautiful and decorative. Today locks and keys infuse our lives in many ways.

Keys can open barriers, granting access to new physical, emotional and spiritual realms. Think of being given "the keys to the city" to welcome an honored guest, or the "key to the heart" as a pledge of love. These modern phrases date back to ancient magical uses when keys became a way to invoke powerful deities. Among the Egyptians Serapis carried the keys to the earth and sky. Early statues of Hecate show her carrying keys said to open the gates of both heaven and the underworld. Janus is portrayed with keys in both of his hands, while Athena holds a key intended to control her city Athens.

In virtually all traditions keys have been accorded great magic and meaning. Handing over the keys of the castle constituted a surrender in Medieval times. In Rome new brides were once given household keys to cement a marriage, while returning the keys would constitute a divorce. Leaving the keys on a spouse's corpse was a way of absolution from debt and other problems incurred by the relationship. In China a favored only child would be given a key to lock him away from death. In Scandinavia large iron keys would be hung over barn doors to protect the cattle, while in Italy tiny decorative keys were given to babies to protect them from convulsions. An iron key placed in a birthing bed was thought to assure an easy delivery. Keys left on a table were thought to generate chaos and trouble in the home. A pair of keys crossed was related to healing. A large key ring was a display of wealth. An old key preferred over a new one is an analogy about selecting a familiar tried and true love over the new.

Keys represent expanded knowledge. It is said Queen Victoria first began the custom of wearing a key around the neck as a pendant. A symbol of mourning, it guarded her heart which was forever locked. Today very old skeleton keys are worn as gothic accessories. Many beautiful keys decorated with precious gems and elaborate filigree are incorporated into contemporary jewelry designs. Such keys are never intended to be used with actual locks. Instead they echo a mystery, inspiring speculation about what the charmed key is intended to lock in — or out.

– GRANIA LING

BLACK LIKE MY SOUL

*When forced to summarize the general theory of relativity
in one sentence: Time and space and gravitation have no
separate existence from matter.* – Albert Einstein

SOMETIMES when asked how I like my coffee, I reply, "Black, like my soul." Of course, the responses I receive vary with the person in question and just how sensitive they might be to things like gallows humor, religious symbolism or mystical connotations, but I suppose my somewhat sardonic remark might merit a bit of an explanation.

In the world of occultism, the color black is generally associated with lead, the planet Saturn and all things Saturnine: death, the number 3, poison and the inevitable march (or retreat) of time. Saturn's astrological title as the "Greater Malefic" might also be blamed for adding even more mass to an already burdensome disposition. Additionally, black is associated with the Qabalistic Sephirah Binah, sphere of the Great Sea or Great Mother, whose imposing roster includes personae as dangerous as Demeter, Ereshkigal, Tiamat and Kali.

Looking beyond the gloom of Erebos, though, we find rich, powerful and fertile areas of exploration. To begin with, the ordering of time allows us to order our lives. To quote Einstein,

"The only reason for time is so that everything doesn't happen at once." Imagine a world without any time. A world where everything happened simultaneously, or is happening simultaneously, since the concept of a past tense would be both untenable and irrelevant. Imagine what a right mess that would be. You can thank the "dark side" that it isn't, so to speak.

There was a trend among the Hermetic mystics of the Renaissance to give dread Saturn a bit of a public relations once-over. They realized Time's necessity, how important it was to have something in place to keep what we now like to call the Space-Time Continuum relatively stable, and just how awe-inspiring such a force had to be. Moving beyond the robe and scythe, our defeated despot of the Titan Wars eventually became associated with "divine melancholy," a term denoting quiet poise, intense study, and deep meditation upon Nature and the mysteries of the Universe.

Visualization time. Gaze deep into the primal ocean, down where only the most frightfully adapted monsters dwell. Using sensing apparati that you or I can only imagine, they grope blindly in a cold inky desert for their next meal, mate, or mutilation. Rise slowly past the near-uncountable schools of sardine, salmon and tuna, the snapping jaws of seals and sharks that fill the waters with blood. The rays and great whales, the millions of mollusks, cephalopods, crustaceans and anemone carpeting the reefs, the mass-spawning that occurs in moonlit shallows. This is Saturn-Binah territory we're speaking of, from whose fertile womb the first creatures ever to inhabit land crawled.

Now imagine a clear night sky. Meditate upon its illimitable darkness. That grim, barren vastness that yet holds trillions of worlds of ice and fire, all of them twirling and dancing to the chaotic cadence of the cosmic void. Saturn-Binah represents the black gulf between the pin-pricks of light, as well as their centers of gravity. The heaviest point of any matter is its center of gravity, yet that is also the point upon which it spins and moves. The Earth's rotation which we experience as days, nights, and seasons (Saturn was known as a deity of agriculture and the harvest), not to mention the revolutions of moons, solar systems and galaxies are all achieved through a series of gravitational axis points. In our own Milky Way, scientists are currently training their telescopes upon what they believe to be a super massive black hole at the galaxy's center, acting as both supreme pivot and cosmic devourer. Saturn-Binah thus signifies both the blackness within which our universe floats, and the myriad balance points upon which its colorful dancers of quasars, gas giants, red dwarfs, asteroids and nebulae twirl.

Tomb. Womb. Mystery.
Time. Space. Gravity.
Saturn. Binah. Black.

How would I like my coffee?
Black like my soul, thank you.
And if you could, please give it a little spin for me.

–Anthony Teth

Velines

Lithuanian death customs and the Day of the Dead

THE LITHUANIANS of both today and yesteryear believed that the soul continued to exist beyond death, visiting the land of the living with consistency. The Day of the Dead concluded a month of celebratory remembrances of the dead in the fall, climaxing on November 2, including some very specific rites meant to pay homage to departed ancestors.

Lithuania is an area of Europe where Pagan connected customs remain strong, even to this day. In fact, this was one of the last bastions to be converted to Christianity, and as a matter of course many church holidays in Lithuania remain infused with Pagan customs and not so distant memories of the past. Although the Day of the Dead is associated with the Catholic calendar, its Lithuanian name Velines is cognate with the name of Velnias, the god who is "the shadow of death"

The world tree

The ancient Balts viewed the world as a tree, with branches reaching up to the sky gods in the heavens and roots reaching deep into the underworld. Velnias lived in the underworld, taking the form of the serpent that coiled around roots of the great cosmic tree, while ruling over the dead. His was not a destitute land, rather it was a land of eternal green and grassy plains, filled with fantastical creatures and the spirits of the deceased. Velnias would often send the spirits of the dead into the world of the living to carry his messages and to bring back the gifts that the living provided for him and those in his domain. The dead were never truly departed, they were just away for a bit.

In order to fully understand the relationship between the living and the dead, let us first look at some of the customs surrounding the death of a family member. Lithuanians believed the soul separated from the body after death, and continued existing among the living, while also living in the land of Velnias. Upon the death of a family member, it fell to the eldest female member of the household to verbally recount the virtues of the deceased. Silence would be maintained in the home of the deceased to show respect for the raging soul, dead except for the recounting of deeds until burial. The ancient Balts knew it was equally important to show their love for the deceased after death as it was during life. It was also highly important that the dead continue to help the family through petition, and the family not lose the relationship by forgetting their worldly deeds.

Two final breaths

If death was preceded by sickness and it was apparent that death was imminent, close relatives and neighbors were informed so that all could help with the process, have time to say farewell, and forgive each other. During the process, it was held that no one should sleep, so as not to be trapped by the soul transitioning. Even the youngest were kept awake.

Dying, according to Lithuanian belief, is the separation of the soul from the body. The soul leaves the body like a mist in two final breaths, first from the chest, and then from the throat. As a person is dying, all windows and doors are opened wide so that the dying person's soul and the familial spirits who came to meet him could fly out freely. The death was immediately announced to all domestic animals — bees were informed by a knock on the hive in order to prevent the departed soul from absconding with all the animals.

Three fistfuls of dirt

Only once the announcements had been made, the deeds had been sung and the body washed and put into a coffin, was the spirit ready for the journey to the land of Velnias. To ease the journey, objects such as tools, family heirlooms and other necessities for the afterlife would be placed into the coffin to help ease the passage. Vestiges of these traditions are found in modern Lithuanian practices of placing pictures of saints, rosaries and other religious articles in the casket. Once in the coffin, the body was taken from the house as expeditiously as possible. The placing of the dead person in the coffin meant the final separation from the living. Leaving a coffin in the house only invites the dead to grab another soul to accompany them on their journey. Once in the grave, it was traditional for a family member to throw three fistfuls of dirt on the coffin in request that the soul of the deceased know peace. Pouring earth three times is an ancient magical ritual meant to chase the soul of the dead person from amongst the living.

Immediately following the internment, the family would hold a dinner in honor of the spirit. This dinner was not only for the recently passed member of the family, rather it was also a celebratory dinner where all the deceased are invited to join in the evening's merriment. Those who attended the dinner

111

would drink a toast to the dead and bid their loved ones a final goodbye, wishing them a pleasant journey. The dinner is also an opportunity to ask Velnias for a blessing. Since the funeral dinner is intended for the souls of the deceased's family, it is not customary for anyone to take any food home with them. It is a common belief that if someone takes little bit of food, then somebody in their family will die soon.

Harvest of souls

The relationship between the dead and the living does not stop with internment. Remembrance of the dead is an annual event in modern Lithuania. The annual harvest marks a shift in psyche: a time to batten down the hatches before the onset of the harshness of the winter and a time to remember what has been harvested, including the harvest of souls by Velnias. Lithuanians would listen for the voice of the dead on the whispering winds over the fields, knowing the gates of eternity were open so those who had passed may join us again.

The festivities for the departed begin when the fields have been cleared and continue until November 2nd. All of the traditions surrounding the celebration of the dead are directly impacted by the fact that it is truly believed that the dead return to this world and, more particularly, to their homes. The dead are received with some trepidation, but more certainly with honor, hospitality and graciousness.

Some of the customs practiced today have their roots in practices that predate the dawn of Christianity in Slavic lands. The sharing of food with the dead was among those customs that have survived from long ago. In the early twentieth century, it was common to bring an assortment of foods to the cemetery to be left on the graves. This was food that was not partaken of by the living, rather it was for the ancestors' consumption.

Funerary meals

Once back in the home, a meal consisting of seven different foods (meat, grains and eggs) was prepared and the table set in a room where all the windows and doors were left open. As in the case of funeral rites, the common belief was by leaving these open, the spirits could come and go more easily.

Once all were gathered around the table, the eldest among the living would pick up a candle and circle it three times around his head and the food. Before partaking of the meal, all would spill a portion of their drink and put a bit of their food on a table set for the dead in the corner of the room. In fact, it was common belief that "the soul of the dead cannot rest if the table is not set." As each shared their portion, he or she would say aloud "No one dared sit at this table, lest they join the realm of the

ancestors." As each put a bit of drink and meal on the table, he or she would say aloud: "This is for you, dear souls".

Once finished with providing a meal for the dead, the living were then invited to stand around the table, while the eldest (usually the father of the household) offered a prayer of remembrance: "Dear souls of the dead, you are still remembered by the members of my family, you are most worthy of our perpetual remembrance, especially you, my grandparents, my parents, also our relatives, children and everyone whom death took away from our home. I invite you to this annual feast. We wish that this feast is agreeable to you, just like memory of all of you, is to us." This prayer would be followed by a short silence, after which all were invited to take a seat and eat. Like the Dumb Supper customs of Western Europe, this was often a meal taken in silence. What better way to hear the dead than to keep your ears perked up for their voices, rather than those of the living?

Spirit sight, special bread

During the meal, it was up to those gifted with the "spirit sight" to look for signs of attendance of the dead. The dead could make an appearance in the steam that rose from food, or the sideways glance of a windows's reflection, or the crackling and groans of ceiling or floorboards. Confirmation with any of these or other signs was a good omen, indicating that the dead were pleased with the proceedings.

Another custom, common at the beginning of the century, was for a special bread to be baked on November 2nd. This bread was not consumed by family members. Rather, each loaf would be named for a specific ancestor and then given to those less fortunate, such as local beggars. The order of naming followed a very specific regimen: naming first the mother of the household, then her father, and so on. Of course, with the passage of time, remembering all the ancestors could be quite a task and one which would invariably leave someone unnamed. To this end, a special loaf would be made, which was dedicated to those souls whose name the baker could not remember.

While there are typical customs, popular among many households, there are certainly also variations of these themes. One particular custom combines both bread baking and the meal. In this custom, the table is set with nine bowls, each containing different foods. A tenth bowl would be set at the head of the table. A spoonful of the contents of the other nine are placed into this tenth bowl. The contents of the tenth bowl would then be mixed with buckwheat flour and other ingredients for the making of bread. This was then fashioned into rolls, one for each deceased ancestor. These rolls, like the loaves mentioned above, would be given to beggars, who would be asked to pray for the dead members of the contributing family.

A galaxy of light

In another variation of the theme, there are some areas where most of the festivities for the dead would take place in the cemetery. In this case, after the religious observance commemorating the souls of the departed, the family would go to the graveside of their beloved ancestors. The evening of convening with the dead would begin with prayers and candles, followed by a meal shared with the dead, right on the grave. In this case, there would not be a separate dish for the dead, nor would libations be given to an empty cup. Instead, the meals would be placed directly on the graves and the libations poured directly onto the ground, so that the dead buried beneath could participate directly (taste!) in the meal. To this very day, on November 2nd, the cemeteries become a galaxy of light with candles constellating the graves of family members. It is believed the candles attract and light the way for wandering souls in the darkness.

Of course, in all cases, when all was said and done, the living would celebrate their own "livingness" by breaking the somber silence of these proceedings by going to a local pub.

Some of the common beliefs regarding the Day of the Dead are:

✳ On All Souls Day, the souls of the dead come to visit the living, asking that the living pray for them.

✳ One time before All Saints' Day, a homemaker swept the house and sprinkled it with sand. In the morning, she saw the floor covered with small footprints, yet there were no small children in the house. Therefore she understood that the souls of dead children had come into the house.

✳ If a mother went to the cemetery at midnight on All Souls' Day, she would see her dead children.

✳ On All Souls' Day, churches are filled with the souls of the dead. That day, these souls are not burning in hell. They are happy. However some souls, whose mothers are wailing, arrive wet, soaked by earthly tears. Thus, there is no need to cry for the dead.

✳ On the Eve of All Saints' Day, one does not go visiting or walking through villages, because all roads and the countryside are filled with the souls of the dead. There may also be some mean souls.

✳ On All Souls' Day and in the evening, no ashes or garbage must be taken out, because the souls can be witched by these items.

✳ If it rains on the night of All Souls' Day, there will be numerous deaths in the following year.

✳ If the sun does not shine on All Saints' Day, the following year will be filled with misfortune.

✳ If trees are still fully covered with leaves on All Saints' Day, it will be a year of Black Death.

✳ If a child is born on the eve of All Souls' Day, then, when in life he attends a funeral meal, he will see evil souls.

– DEMETRIUS SANTIAGO

AN IMPERFECT CAKE

WHEN I LOOK BACK on my childhood, it seems as if all the happy memories blend into one. The dizzy excitement of Christmas morning. The smell of Thanksgiving turkey, fresh from the oven. Sleeping in a little later on the first day of school vacation. Rushing from house to house on Halloween night clutching a paper bag filled with treats. And best of all, for me at least, blowing out candles on a birthday cake, while making a wish.

Each single moment, once experienced uniquely, becomes a thread of memory woven into a tapestry of shared human experience. In the end, if we're lucky, we can pull the tapestry over us like a blanket on a cold winter's night. The individual vignettes that make up our lives become less important than knowing that, in the final edit, we are safe and warm and happy.

By contrast, the difficult moments in our lives often assume an almost epic place in our memory. They refuse to blend in and they defy generalization. This brings me to a bright October morning many years ago in a small Pennsylvania town.

A magical October day

To say it was a magical day may seem silly, but then again, all October days are magical to some degree: bright leaves on the trees, the smell of wood smoke in the air, and the promise of Halloween — the most fantastic day of the year — only a few short weeks away. But this October day was my birthday.

We lived in a modest household. There were four children. I seldom saw my father. He worked long days in a factory to provide for his family, leaving for work before I was awake and arriving home exhausted long past my bedtime.

My mother, like most women of her era, was a professional housewife. She cooked and cleaned and did the laundry. She nursed us back to health when we were sick. She tucked us in at night and shook us gently awake in the morning, so as not to miss the school bus. Money was always hard-earned, but we never went to sleep without food in our bellies.

Small sacrifices

Throughout the year, Mom would save money for each of our birthdays. A dollar here, a few coins there, put discreetly out of sight into a cardboard shoe box. When our birthdays arrived, we were magically granted two wishes: she would cook whatever we wanted for dinner and she would order a birthday cake with our name on it from the local bakery.

While my siblings often asked for things like steak or barbecue for dinner, I always asked for the same thing — picnic sandwiches and potato chips. I'd work side by side with my mother in the kitchen assembling the sandwiches. I always insisted that we eat them off paper plates instead of the regular dishes.

I don't remember how old I was this particular year. I do remember that when it was time to pick up the cake, I sat in the car next to my mother, while she drove down the narrow mountain road to the town below. We parked in the town lot which was separated from Main Street by a twin set of railroad tracks that carried freight cars filled with coal from the local mines to the steel mills farther down river.

There was no easy way to get to the shops. One had to step carefully over the tracks to reach the other side, after first making certain that there were no trains approaching in either direction. We made it across the tracks without a hitch and my mother and I were soon standing in the bakery. "It's my son's birthday," she announced proudly, "We've come to pick up his cake."

An autumn-colored cake

Then suddenly, there it was! All sugar and spun frosting, in the autumn colors my mother insisted upon. Orange and yellow and red frosting; a proper October cake. Seeing the look on my face, the clerk brought the cake down to my eye level.

"Is that your name?" he asked, to which I nodded enthusiastically, so breathless with excitement that I could not speak. He placed the cake carefully in a large cardboard box while my mother counted out the dollar bills she had tucked away over many months. When the transaction was completed, I asked my mother if I could carry the cake. I think I meant it as more of a chivalrous gesture than anything else, but she happily agreed.

Out of the store we went, walking slowly down the street toward the parking lot, side by side, my mother and me. When we reached the railroad tracks, there was a freight train rattling by us. I was holding the cake and her hand rested on my shoulder. We waited together patiently for the train to pass.

The tracks of my tears

When the caboose finally rolled past me, I stepped instinctively onto the train tracks and started across. My mother followed behind. I'm not exactly sure how it happened — I suspect a shoe lace had come undone — but my foot suddenly twisted beneath

me and I fell onto the railroad tracks, crushing the cardboard box and its precious contents.

My mother, more concerned about my welfare than the cake's, picked me up and dusted me off, making sure that there was no permanent damage. Luckily, I was fine. My birthday cake was not as fortunate.

I don't remember fussing a lot. I didn't ask for another cake, because I understood, at an early age, the little sacrifices made throughout the year to make this single moment possible.

So we picked up what was left of the cake and went home.

But there is a candle

Later that night, as my brothers complained about having to eat sandwiches for dinner, I helped myself to a finger full of icing from the inside of the cake box and resolved to put the memory of the imperfect cake behind me forever.

My mother, sensing my disappointment, sat down beside me. "You still get a wish you know," she smiled.

"But there's no cake."

"But there is a candle," she responded, pulling one from the pocket of her house dress.

"But there's no fire," I responded.

"Use your imagination."

Rules of wish craft

I remember sitting there for what seemed like hours, staring at the candle that she held patiently in front of my nose, trying to see a flame where there was none. Like most kids, I believed that birthday wishes are acts of magic. They do come true if you follow the rules:

Never take the wish lightly. Blow out all the candles with a single breath. Do not speak the wish out loud. Do not doubt — not even for an instant — and never tell anyone what you wished for. Ever.

"You do believe in magic, don't you?" she asked quietly. I nodded my head yes.

"Then blow out the candle." I closed my eyes, drew a deep breath, and exhaled.

I can't honestly remember the wish. I'd like to think it was for another cake, more fabulous than the last one or for more wishes, as many as I could make in a single breath. But I think what I actually wished for was to fall asleep and not remember the day at all when I woke up. How ironic that now it's the only childhood birthday I remember.

– JIMAHL DI FIOSA

The Zodiac and Cell Salts

Astrological secrets for good health

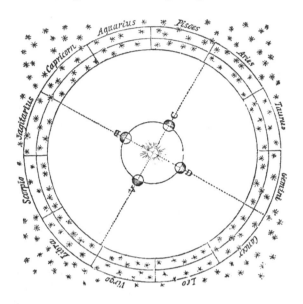

HEALTH, WEALTH and happiness! Sometimes called The Three Keys, this trinity of treasures is a legendary formulae for unlocking destiny's door to a fulfilling life. Health comes first and foremost. Perhaps this is because it might be the most precious key of all. For thousands of years astrological consultations have included information regarding health care. In earlier times physicians were also accomplished astrologers. Dr. Nicholas Culpeper, the famed 17th Century healer, wrote a medical guide based upon herbal cures related to the planets. His work is still consulted today by witches and others who would turn to natural medicines to enhance wellness.

The zodiac's twelve cell salts, one for each astrological sign, are safe and effective tools to use in conjunction with the horoscope for healing. The twelve cell salts are derived from various minerals which occur naturally. They are essential to growth and wellness in plants as well as in the diets of animals and human beings. Cell salts can be consumed in trace amounts in foods. They can also be purchased strengthened as highly purified compounds in the form of tiny sweet tasting pills. Look for cell salts among the vitamins and homeopathic remedies where health foods are sold.

Gentle and safe, cell salts are not drugs. Everyone, including children and the elderly, can benefit from taking

♈ ♉ ♊ ♋ ♌ ♍ ♎ ♏ ♐ ♑ ♒ ♓

them. Just a minimal grasp of astrology is needed to select the proper cell salts to facilitate healing. Begin by considering only the familiar Sun sign we all know. The various birth signs indicate the ailments an individual might be prone to according to the part of the body linked to that zodiac sign. For example, Aries rules the head and brain. Aries people can be prone to headaches and depression. Taurus rules the ears and throat, so that area can be vulnerable. It is said we use more of the cell salt linked to the birth sign than any other. Replenishing just that cell salt alone can aid in overcoming many deficiencies and result in improved health.

Those with a deeper background in astrology can include the cell salts related to the ascendant and 6th house. In the horoscope these are the rulers of the physical body and overall health conditions.

– DIKKI-JO MULLEN

119

THE TWELVE CELL SALTS OF THE ZODIAC

THESE ARE the twelve cell salts along with their related zodiac signs and parts of the body. The foods included contain trace amounts of the various cell salts.

Aries
Potassium phosphate, K_3PO_4
Food Sources: carrots, garlic, milk, bran, buttermilk, dates, parsley, beans, mustard greens, beets, peppers, avocado, cheese and wheat germ
Body part: head and brain cells

Taurus
Sodium sulfate, Na_2SO_4
Food Sources: rosemary, lettuce, kohlrabi, milk, celery, onions, eggs, cabbage, Brussels sprouts, chard, spinach and radishes
Body Part: ears and throat

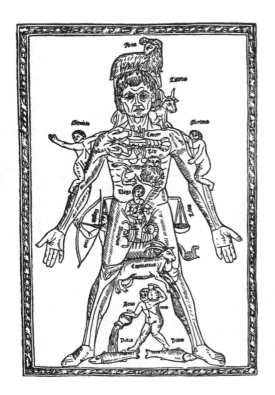

Gemini
Potassium chloride, KC_1
Food Sources: strawberries, coconuts, radishes, parsley, lentils, blueberries, asparagus, cottage cheese, pineapple, sauerkraut, cucumbers and asparagus
Body part: arms and hands

Cancer
Calcium fluoride, CaF
Food Sources: carrots, turnips, cabbage, goat cheese, kale, kelp, pineapple and watercress
Body Part: breast and stomach

Leo
Magnesium phosphate, $Mg_3(PO_4)_2$
Food Sources: soybeans, beechnuts, limes, lemons, oranges, plums, gooseberries, grapefruit, wild rice, cashews, cherries and figs
Body Part: heart, lungs and back

Virgo
Potassium sulfate, K_2SO_4
Food Sources: onions, avocados, cucumbers, Brazil nuts, cauliflower, dill, peaches, tomatoes, green beans, licorice, celery and fennel
Body Part: lower digestive tract, also nervous disorders

Libra
Sodium phosphate, Na_3PO_4
Food Sources: whole wheat, buttermilk, peas, citrus fruits and juices, coconut, asparagus, acorns, brown rice, parsley,

dandelion greens, lentils, eggs, cottage cheese and sunflower seeds
Body Part: kidneys and lower back

Scorpio
Calcium sulfate, $CaSO_4$
Food Sources: milk, egg yolks, lettuce, radishes, onions, turnips, kohlrabi, currants, cauliflower, horehound, cabbage and horseradish
Body Part: reproductive system and lower bowels

Sagittarius
Silicon dioxide, SiO_2
Food Sources: Shredded Wheat, strawberries, carrots, cucumber skins, endive, rye flour, oats, peas, chicory, gooseberries and black pepper
Body Part: hips and upper legs, blood pressure and blood sugar levels

Capricorn
Calcium phosphate, $Ca_3(PO_4)_2$
Food Sources: beets, beans, peanuts, almonds, cheese, avocados, linseed meal, pistachios, carrots, wintergreen, buttermilk and comfrey.
Body part: knees, skeletal structure, skin

Aquarius
Sodium chloride, $NaCl$
Food Sources: apples, seaweed, pecans, peaches, spinach, egg yolks, Swiss chard, onions, Roquefort and goat cheeses, beets, tomatoes, mangos, figs and water chestnuts.
Body Part: ankles and the circulatory system

Pisces
Iron phosphate, Fe_3PO_4
Food Sources: kidney beans, apricots, brewer's yeast, pumpkin, soybeans, tofu, bok choy, raisins, collard greens, molasses, spinach, lentils, enriched breads and cereals, sauerkraut and chamomile
Body Part: the feet

– DIKKI-JO MULLEN

❖ Breaking Glass ❖

SEVEN YEARS of bad luck. That's the first thing that pops into most of our heads when we break a mirror. But what if you break plain glass?

The superstition that breaking a mirror is bad luck stems from the ancient Greek belief that one's soul is reflected in a mirror. The Romans added the assertion that the bad luck would last for seven years, as they believed that life is split into seven-year cycles.

Touch wood

But even in populations that believe that breaking mirrors is bad luck, people often believe that breaking any other kind of glass is good luck, especially if it's clear glass. The glass absorbs and dissipates the bad energy meant for you, causing the glass to break. For example, in some parts of Italy, it is perceived that the *malocchio* (Evil Eye) was given, but the glass absorbed the charge, thus deflecting the hex.

Some cultures use apotropaic magic to ensure that the evil is dissipated. Apotropaic, from the Greek meaning to ward off and to turn away, is a type of magic used to deflect misfortune. You use this yourself when you knock on wood ("touch wood" in the UK) to avert tempting fate when you say something boastful.

On its head

In some parts of Germany, when a person breaks glass, he or she says *Scherben bringen Glück!* meaning "the shards [of broken glass] will bring you luck." In parts of Serbia, a person will say *Na njegovu glavu!* (on its head), meaning "may the evil be upon the head" of the thing just broken.

If a glass or plate falls off a wall by itself, though, it means that someone you know has died. If the glass is part of a framed photograph or painting of a person, it means bad luck for the person in the photo, possibly even that the person will die soon. Another belief, attributed to Great Britain, says that if you look through a piece of broken glass at anyone, you will have a quarrel with that person.

Shard reading

So how do you know if your glass-breaking is good luck or bad? You can always use divination. As in a tea leaf reading, look at the shapes.

Do the shards suggest anything to you? Hearts? Animals? A face? A scene? If there is a triangular-shaped piece, in which direction is it pointing? That may indicate from which direction the luck is coming. If you see animals, do they look threatening or friendly? This, and the groupings of the glass can reveal what thoughts lie hidden in your subconscious, similar to how a Rorschach (ink blot) test works.

So next time glass breaks, take notice. It could be a good omen.

– MORVEN WESTFIELD

Merry Meetings

A candle in the window, a fire on the hearth,
a discourse over tea...

THIS YEAR WE had the pleasure of visiting with David Conway, a mystic, magus and author whose profound knowledge, unique insights and clear writing style have affected Literary Esoterica since the early 70s. The seventh child of a seventh child, David was reared in the seaside city of Aberystwyth, Wales and its surrounding environs. His education in magic began at a very early age, studying with a local farmer, Mr. James, a magician he encountered in the Welsh countryside before embarking on his own inner journey.

David brought magical training to the forefront publishing *Magic: An Occult Primer* very early in his adult life. This very same tome would prove to be the "go to" treatise for magicians beginning their own journey into sublime realms. Colin Wilson in his foreword to this very same text exclaimed, "There is nothing of the phoney or the exhibitionist about David Conway. He is not merely a magician, but a genuine mystic, an intensely private person who is absorbed in what Blake called the inner worlds and their mystery..."

In the mundane world, David earned a diplomatic posting to Brussels, as well as assumed the role of Principal Director of the European Patent Office in Munich. He has also worked as a civil servant in London, and has since retired to the Welsh countryside where he continues his inner work.

What prompted you to write your very first book, Magic: an Occult Primer? There were other books on magic around at the time – Dion Fortune, Crowley, and Regardie for example – but your own adopts a more practical, hands-on approach, even though you cover theoretical aspects as well.

When I wrote that first book I was in my early twenties and fresh from college. My aim was to offer my contemporaries an introduction to magic that didn't pull its punches. You see most of the books available then – and there weren't all that many – struck me as terribly old-fashioned. I have in mind not just their style or their language – and here I exempt Dion Fortune whose prose I admire – but also their irritating coyness. Irritating because the writer would hint at great mysteries but stop short, well short, of disclosing what they were. A bit like Gypsy Rose Lee who promised to bare all but never did: it kept punters on the edge of their seats but in the end they went home short-changed.

That's why I included in the book two complete rituals and invited, nay challenged, readers to try one or both for themselves. In retrospect I'm a little shocked by that. But those were times when young people wanted to try things out for themselves, not be told about them by others. And, happily, no one to my knowledge ever came to grief. On the contrary, hundreds of people wrote to say they'd had their first experience of magic by following my instructions and were impatient to learn more. (I replied to every letter. Indeed my first batch of royalties went on stationery and stamps!) That said, I'm sufficiently realistic to know that the credit for whatever readers got out of the book lay with them, not with me. All I'd done was help them discover their magical potential.

As for the authors you mention, yes, their work was in print but inaccessible, often unknown, to people unfamiliar with the specialist bookshops that stocked them. My advantage was to be accepted by a mainstream publisher and so benefit from the superior resources – distribution, publicity and market presence – such companies can offer. Two years earlier Paul Huson's Mastering Witchcraft *had enjoyed similar benefits, but for the moment I can think of no other. Interestingly enough, Paul Huson was also in his early twenties when he wrote his book. We were the enfants terribles of occultism, looked down upon by the Old Guard. This, I suspect, was because we happened to be young and a wee bit cheeky. Plus we sold a lot of books.*

To jump from your first book to the most recent…

That's a big jump. Almost a lifetime. You make me feel my age!

It's a gap of forty years. And as you say, none of us is getting younger! Anyway, early on in your most recent book, Magic Without Mirrors – which is in large part the story of your life – you mention a family connection to various occultists. Can you say more about that?

Well, let me explain that the connection was a social one, nothing more. You see, my mother's parents were friendly with those of Dion Fortune, in those days a young and, by all accounts, rather serious little girl named Violet Mary Firth. This was at Llandudno in North Wales. The Firths lived on the road leading to a promontory called the Little Orme, while my mother's family had a house on its larger rival, the Great Orme, at the opposite end of the bay. And then by coincidence my father later got to know Dion Fortune's husband, Thomas Penry Evans, though by then he'd remarried. I remember he and his second wife used sometimes to call at our house when I was small. Family legend – and it may be no more than that – maintains that one day he predicted I'd be a magician when I grew up.

In the event I was introduced to magic long before I grew up, thanks to another friend of my father's, someone I knew only as Mr. James. (Long afterwards I learned his first name was Mathonwy.) From an early age I'd spend every Saturday on his farm in the mountains behind the small town where I grew up. There was no formal initiation or anything – such an event would have scared the living daylights out of me and, I'm sure, embarrassed him no end as well. Instead he explained, in terms a young boy like me could understand, what magic was all about and, more importantly, how to practice it.

Wales has a long tradition of myth and magic. Did this nourish and inform your development?

Oh certainly. Remember, too, that Welsh was my first language, indeed my only language, until the age of six. As a child I grew up on Celtic folklore, particularly that of my native Wales. It has informed and shaped my magical development. One result is that the cosmology I learned as a boy, to take one example, was expressed in terms of Celtic myth, yet I quickly discovered that in essence it was not dissimilar to, say, the Kabbalah or any other system. All traditions, after all, endeavour to describe a common truth, one which is,

of its very nature, inexpressible. It can only be experienced. Or, if you like, it can only be lived.

What you describe is a sort of one-to-one tuition. Would it be fair to suggest that, so far as magic is concerned, you've remained a "loner", rather than a "joiner", by which I mean you've never belonged to a particular group or society?

Well, I was an only child and, despite having friends, soon became accustomed to my own company, as only children do. I was an avid reader and by the time I met Mr. James, already borrowing books on the supernatural from our local library, a pretty eclectic – at times eccentric – mix, ranging from Eliphas Levi to Gerald Gardner and from Lord Dowding, a committed Spiritualist, to Alice Bailey. (Admittedly I did find Mrs. Bailey something of a challenge!) So yes, I suppose I was

a loner. And because of that, as well as the one-to-one training I received, I may have retained a tendency to regard magic as a private affair, at least much of the time. That's not in any way to diminish the merits of working in a group. On the contrary "more" may well mean "better," thanks to the collective effort and the synergic effect it produces. There's no hard and fast rule. We're all different. What suits one best is what works best each time.

But you asked if I'd ever joined a group or society. In the late nineteen-eighties I was persuaded to join the Anthroposophical Society but didn't stay long. And I still send off my annual subscription to the Theosophical Society, even though I regard Madame Blavatsky as a rogue as well as a genius. A lovable rogue nevertheless.

Would you call yourself a ceremonial magician?

The term "ceremonial" scares me slightly. It sounds a little pompous. That said, ceremony has an important place in magic – and my first book encouraged readers to indulge in it – but we should bear in mind that ceremony is the means to an end. If, for instance, wearing special clothes or, for that matter, no clothes at all, has the effect of detaching one from one's everyday environment, even one's everyday self, then so much the better. The same is true of the "correspondences" appropriate to a specific intention or the choreography of a particular rite. If, on the other hand, pomp and circumstance are indulged in for their own sake, then

a fancy-dress party is a better place to be in than a magic circle. It may be fun, but it's not magic.

What I'm saying is that of itself ceremony is unmagical. Where magical power resides – and both Crowley and Dion Fortune made the point – is in an act of will. Ceremony, private or collective, may fortify the will and focus its direction, but it won't replace it. On top of which, with practice, the will can be trained to function no less efficiently without external help. Which is perhaps why I'm nowadays less fond of the term "ceremonial magician" than I used to be, at least so far as concerns myself.

You are, I know, close, very close, to several prominent figures in contemporary witchcraft, as well as in the pagan movement generally. Would you regard yourself as a pagan?

All I've just said about magic is, I suggest, applicable to witchcraft, druidry and much else. The externals may vary from one type of practice to the next – and that's true even within, say, witchcraft – but the essentials remain the same. As an Oxford don, a distinguished Kabbalist, once told me – the modus operandi may vary but the operatio it serves seldom does.

But you asked if I'm a pagan.

It depends what you mean by the word. Readers of the Almanac won't need reminding that it derives from the Latin paganus ("rural" or "rustic"), a term applied by early Christians, often town or city dwellers, to country folk not yet converted to the one true god. Instead pagans favoured not one god but many, each manifesting itself in (or, rather, through) the world around them. To me this concept is fundamental to the practice of magic so, yes, I am a pagan.

It allows us, after all, to suppose a divine presence in the very fabric of the universe – what Spinoza called "immutable substance" and Hegel "the absolute reality of spirit." Yet it falls short, well short, of pantheism. There, the divine is totally absorbed in Nature, whereas for pagans it manifests itself in the world, while also existing outside it. And because we, too, are part and parcel of the world, it is necessarily present in us. This is why Plato could argue that though subject to change, temporality and contingency, human beings have an inherent dynamism towards the Absolute, a faculty that enables them to discern in themselves and in their surroundings the presence of an all-embracing cosmic being.

Our ancestors understood this perfectly. Dismissed nowadays as simple-minded nature worshippers because they identified their gods and goddesses with specific places – islands, lakes, mountains and rivers – or with natural phenomena, what they were doing was detecting in their environment the divine presence to which it bore witness. This enabled them, like modern pagans, to have access to a supernatural reality to which we likewise belong. It was described by the German philosopher, Hegel, as the ultimate form of Unity, one whose components have no meaning other than their unity, while that unity has no meaning other than its parts. What that means is that the totality of being is both many in one and one in many something the Emperor Julian, the last pagan emperor, made plain to his critics in the 4th Century of our era. His commitment to polytheism was unflinching but he never lost sight of the "One" that encompasses the "many" Neither should contemporary pagans. In their ritual practice, they may treat as real a variety of gods and goddesses, and rightly so, but few, if asked, would deny that these are but expression of the One they ultimately represent.

Oops. I've waffled on too much. And I risk giving the impression of being serious, even slightly pompous. I assure you I'm not. For me, magic has always been fun. Were it not so, I'd have abandoned it years ago. Instead of which, it has been part, probably the defining part, of my entire life. That's why, in my latest book, I sought to share that life with others, the serious bits and, still more, the fun bits as well.

THE FIRE OF THE GODS

HUMANKIND emerged from our unknown evolutionary past with the special aid of several natural things. Humankind's awakening minds would have reached out to the natural world as the very presence and power that sustains life. The shelter of stone and tree, the core need for running water, all the allies that feed us: all these would have been the object of our spiritual seeking. Of all the core powers that we must have known as our minds emerged, there is a special place for the remarkable power of fire.

Wild Fire, Tame Fire

In the first days, fire must have been wild. Lightning brings it to dry grass; the sun strikes properly through a drop of water; and the hungry power rises. Pain accompanies it, but so does light and warmth, the feast of cooked food, and the most remarkable feast for the eyes a proto-human was likely to see. The word 'divine' derives from roots that mean 'shining' and ancient Vedic lore speaks of the Three Great Lights – the Sun, Moon, and Fire.

Ancient myth and story speaks of mortals stealing fire from the gods. The Greeks told of the Titan Prometheus, whose name means 'forethought', who stole fire from the great hearth of the gods on Olympus. He brought this to Earth and taught mortals how to tend and keep it and how to sacrifice to the gods. Among European Pagan peoples, almost all meat eaten at meals was killed by sacrifice to the gods. It was the sacred fire stolen from the sky or the burning forest by clever skill and courage that gave mortals the gift of cooked food. Forevermore, it was cooked food that was offered, in turn, to the gods and spirits in Pagan religious rites.

Hearth Fire, Sacred Fire

In European pre-Christian religions, both fire in the sacred temples and fire in the hearth of the home were sacred. The keeping of the hearth-fire was the center of women's cult in the ancient world, with a complex of seasonal customs, cleansings, maintenance and relighting. Keeping the hearth clean and pure insured the luck and growth of the family — to allow the fire to lose its spark was a bad omen indeed.

The fire lit in religious rituals was brought to the temple from a hearth-fire. Temples to the gods in the ancient world often had raised fire-altars set before beautiful images, on which offerings of wine, honey, bread and meat were burned. Sacred ritual fire was the central symbol of divine presence in traditional ways from India, through Persia, and into Greece, Rome and further on into Europe. While the rituals of the ancient Druids are unknown to us, folklore and custom suggests that fire-worship was central to Celtic Paganism.

Fire was used to ritually claim land for a tribe or family. Ancient Greek colonists carried with them sacred fire from their home city and lit a new fire in their distant hearth to claim the land. Centuries later, Irish popular law required that fire be kindled on a property before it was considered properly owned by those who claimed it. Even today, when we go to the forest at night, we light a fire in the center of our camp, and claim the little circle of its light as our own.

Rites and Customs

Getting and keeping fire is surrounded by custom and tradition, continuing all the way into the sorcery of the instruction books of magic known as grimoires. What began as the great fire altar on which food offerings to the gods were burned, became the witch's fire at the center of the dancing-circle. In the ritual magician's circle, it became the consecrated brazier on which offerings of incense and brandy were made. In every case, the proper building and kindling of the fire were of central importance.

The concept of the purity of fire was central. The place where the flame was kindled needed to be clean and orderly. Hearths were swept clean and washed with pure water. The carrying of water from a sacred spring to the hearth was a ritual event for the Vestal Virgins and for hearth keepers all over the Pagan world. Some traditions required complex designs and figures to be drawn in colored powders where the fire would be built, making even the stones of the fire-platform or altar sacred.

While hearth fire was kept in houses, the sacred fire of Pagan ritual was usually lit on raised stone or brick altars. The word 'altar' means 'high place,' and refers primarily to the raised pillar of brick or stone on which the sacrificial fire was built. The sacred fire was always lit from a pure and true hearth fire, one spark that lit both the common home and the high places of the gods.

129

Celtic Fire

Many of the customs that are common in modern Pagan and witchcraft circles can be found in the countryside customs of early-modern Irish and Scots people. The hearth fire was carefully kept by each housewife. To allow the fire to go out or the hearth to be dirty or unswept was to attract ill-luck. To give away a spark of the fire of your hearth to another was to risk giving away the luck of the house.

In Ireland, the custom was to extinguish the hearth fires of every house and relight them on the feast days of Samhain and Beltaine, the days that separated the two halves of the year: summer and winter. In the landscape of Ireland's small isle, the high places where the sacred fires were re-lit were visible for miles. The dark land would be relit by the light spreading from the ancient sites, lit by the rites and songs of the Wise Ones. The luck of the house depended on a good fire. Twice yearly, every home could begin again, with a spark from the fire of a king.

Fire also played a part in practical magical rites. In the Scottish Highlands, if a plague came on the cattle the folk would light the need-fire. Here is an excerpt from the Carmina Gadelica, a compendium of old Gaelic lore, recorded, translated, and edited by folklorist, Alexander Carmichael (1832-1912):

Tein-igin, neid-fire, need-fire, forced fire, fire produced by the friction of wood or iron against wood.... The neid-fire was resorted to in imminent or actual calamity upon the first day of the quarter, and to ensure success in great or important events.

The writer conversed with several persons who saw the neid-fire made, and who joined in the ceremony. ... a woman in Arran said that her father, and the other men of the townland, made the neid-fire on the knoll on 'La buidhe Bealltain' — Yellow Day of Beltane. They fed the fire from 'cuaile mor conaidh caoin' — great bundles of sacred faggots brought to the knoll on Beltane Eve. When the sacred fire became kindled, the people rushed home and brought their herds and drove them through and round the fire of purification...

That was in the second decade of the nineteenth century.

John Macphail, Middlequarter, North Uist, said that (when) the .. snow lay deep and remained long on the ground (it) caused much want and suffering throughout the Isles.

The people of North Uist extinguished their own fires and generated a purification fire... The fire was produced from an oak log by rapidly boring with an auger. This was accomplished by the exertions of ... nine nines of first-begotten sons. From the neid-fire produced on the knoll the people of the parish obtained fire for their dwellings. Many cults and ceremonies were observed ... in which Pagan and Christian beliefs intermingled.

So we see that, even beyond the seasonal re-lightings, fires might be extinguished and re-lit to reclaim luck or drive away ill-fortune.

The famous Irish Druid Mog Ruith or Roith used magical fire as a weapon in a magical war:

The final showdown between two sets of druids, who each make up druidical fires to confound the other side.

Mog Roith tells Fiacha's men each to bring a handful of rowan-wood, while Fiacha himself is to bring a bundle of wood from the side of the mountain which has grown in the shade of three shelters: from the wind of March, from the wind from the sea and from the wind that causes forest fires. The firewood is carefully built up in the shape of a churn with three sides and angles and seven doors. Cormac's fire, however, is roughly stacked and has only three doors.

The fire is ready,' said Cennmar, 'Now it only needs lighting.' Mog Roith struck his tinder-box. Now the fire of the North was also ready, but all were filled with doubt and anxious haste. Mog Roith said to the Munstermen, 'Quickly, each shave a sliver of wood from your spear-handles.' They did so and gave them to him. He then made a mixture of these with butter and laid the ball on the fire, chanting the while:

I mix a roaring, fierce fire,
Clearing woods, blighting grass,
Angry flame of powerful speed,

Rushing to skies above,
Subduing other fires' wrath,
Breaking battle on Conn's race [the North].

Tossed into the fire's heart, the ball lit with a great flame and great uproar. Mog Roith chanted:
God of druids, My God above All other gods...

'Now,' said Mog Roith, 'bring my oxen and ready my chariot; hold your horses ready. If the fires turn towards the North, you must be ready to charge. If this happens, do not delay in charging, as I will do myself. If the fires come from the North, prepare to defend yourselves...'

As he said this, he sent a druidic wind into the atmosphere and into the heavens, so that it formed itself into a shadowy, dark obscurity over Cenn Claire, from which a rain of blood fell.

Mog Roith is successful in turning the flames northwards.

Cormac concedes defeat and the Munstermen, under Mog Roith's guidance, are victorious.

Sorcerer's Fire

The arts that we know as 'magic' were part and parcel of religion and spirituality in the ancient world. As the Christian political church outlawed every ancient sect, traditional rites moved from temples to private homes, and ritual styles adapted. What remained of ancient rites, hidden from the law, became 'occultism' in Christian Europe and in our time.

The question of what real inheritance the modern Pagan and magical movement can claim from the ancients is complex. However, we can trace a fairly direct route of literary inheritance from the technical ritual manuals of the late Classical world through early medieval manuals of spirit contact and at last into the grimoires — the simplified books of magical instruction known to us from the early modern era. Such books as *The Lesser Key of Solomon, The Grimoirium Verum*, and *The Grand Grimoire* are the product of a line of inheritance from the ancient Pagan world, stretched thin though it may be. Transmitted along that thin line is that central symbol of the ancient temple — the ritual fire.

Among the array of the sorcerer's tools, the brazier or fire-bowl is always present. Some writers give instructions for what sort of wood the charcoal is to be made from and most give prayers specific to the lighting of the fire. The ritual fire is then used to make offerings to the spirits called to in the rites, whether to 'God' or to the various lower spirits that appear in magician's books. Often the instruction is to pour brandy onto the fire, but of course properly-formulated incenses are also used. Some of the spirits whose names and signs are given in the grimoires are given specific offerings.

Kindling Sacred Fire

If you would like to bring this custom of sacred fire into your own Pagan ritual work, you will need to observe three rules. The fire must be made of proper materials, kindled in the right way and time, and with proper words.

Sacred fire should be built of well-dried hardwood, with aromatic woods if possible. In the East, sandalwood is often used, but in Northern Europe oak and ash were of central importance; whereas in Ireland the rowan or mountain ash was given magical power in the stories. If you cannot get enough of a specific wood for a full fire, you can kindle the first flames with the symbolic wood and then build it with whatever good dry fuel is available.

Tradition requires that the ritual fire be kept pure. That means keeping it free of trash, picnic debris, discarded food, and so forth. The ritual fire is the presence of power and should be kept sacred. Everything that is put into it, either before or after it is lit, should be deliberate and meaningful. It is not a place to throw trash.

The most traditional way to light sacred fire is by friction. It is perhaps also the most difficult. One can buy a commercial fire-bow kit and give it a try, but be sure to have some practice before planning to use it for ritual fire-lighting. Equally traditional, although less common, is kindling the fire by a burning-lens or curved mirror. In choosing the proper time, sunset or dawn is certainly the best, although noon (the real half-way point between sunrise and set) or midnight are also traditional.

In our modern times, I often choose to not use any 'flint and steel' in kindling a fire – that means no lighters. Using good wooden matches forces us to pay attention to the work. Having worked out of doors in many seasons, my personal superstition is to light the fire with no more than nine matches.

A Fire-Lighting Charm

There are many modern versions of this old Gaelic incantation for lighting a proper fire. I offer mine for your use, and may you be blessed in it.

We kindle this Fire in the presence
*   of the Mighty Ones*
In the name of the Gods of Fire
In the name of the Goddesses of fire
Beneath the lights of Sun and Moon.

Without malice, without envy, without
*   jealousy, without fear,*
Without terror of anything
*   under the sun*
And the Holy Son of the Mother
*   to shield us.*
Kindle you in our hearts, within,
A flame of wisdom, strength and love
To our foes, to our friends,
*   to our kindred all*
To the brave, to the knave, to the thrall
From the lowliest things that liveth
To the names that are highest of all.
Sacred Fire, be present on our hearth
*   and in our hearts!*

Keeping sacred fire brings us close to the ways of the ancients. The pleasure of company at the fire extends from friends and family to tribe and to the gods and spirits themselves. So I wish you well. As it says in the Vedas, one of humankind's oldest scriptures: "May we pray with a good fire."

– IAN CORRIGAN

Tomb Sweeping Day

A Chinese festival of the dead

EACH SPRING, on the fifteenth day following the Spring Equinox (typically April 4, 5 or 6), highway tolls in mainland China are suspended to make travel more affordable. Millions of people anticipate this annual journey, which is rooted in a tradition that began over 2500 years ago. The Chinese government reinstated the Qingming festival in 2008 and officially these people are taking time to go outside and revel in the greenery, while absorbing the wholesome energies of springtime.

Qingming, the name of the festival, may be translated as Pure Brightness Day, Clear Bright Festival as well as Ancestors Day or Tomb Sweeping Day. However, while enjoying the outdoors and 'treading the greenery' as  they are officially encouraged to do, some may also discreetly seek a spiritual awakening. They honor, remember and connect with their departed loved ones. Tombs and burial grounds are swept free of leaves and other debris left by the passing winter. Gifts of food, libations of wine and tea, chopsticks, flowers, candles, joss (lucky burnt paper votive offerings), incense and firecrackers are presented to the deceased. Tomb Sweeping Day has elements reminiscent of both Halloween and Spring Equinox. It honors the processes of death, as well as the promise of rebirth. Chinese communities not under Communist control including those in Taiwan, Hong Kong, Vietnam and Malaysia are able to express the religious elements of Qingming. They celebrate their ancestors more openly.

This beautiful and bittersweet tradition, originally called Hanshi Day, might have begun as a memorial in 636 BCE when Jie Zitui died. He was a loyal follower of Duke Wen. Jie supported the duke during a difficult nineteen year exile. Once, when the duke was starving, Jie saved him by serving a nourishing soup. As he relished the delicious soup, Duke Wen was most appreciative, but could not understand how Jie found the ingredients to make it. It turned out that Jie had sliced off and stewed a piece of his own thigh. Duke Wen was so touched that he promised Jie a handsome reward. Jie sought no reward: he only wanted to help Wen become king.

Upon ascending the throne, Wen rewarded many loyal followers, but Jie disappeared into the forest, not seeking compensation. He had merely wanted to help Wen. Determined to find him,

Wen ordered the forest burned down in order to force Jie to come out of hiding. However, Jie perished in the fire. Overcome by remorse, Wen ordered the people to honor Jie by going three days without fire. Wen also established a place held sacred to his benefactor, naming it Jiexiu, meaning "the place where Jie rests forever." At first, the faithful would sacrifice a live rooster annually to honor Jie's death. Later, the holy day expanded to include other offerings to all of those who were mourned.

Another tradition credits the origin of Qingming to the Tang Emperor Xuanzong. In 732 CE, this emperor declared that Chinese citizens were becoming wasteful and extravagant. Ostentatious ancestor-worshipping ceremonies were being held too often and were used to try to outshine everyone else. The emperor declared that such parties could only take place on the one-hundred-fourth day after the Winter Solstice, which is also the fifteenth day following the Spring Equinox.

The Qingming festival has been firmly rooted in Chinese culture ever since. Family members of all ages gather to sweep tombs and have a party for their ancestors. This has expanded to include dancing, singing, and flying beautiful paper kites to honor and delight those who have passed away. Often willow branches are placed near household gates and doorways at the end of the day for protection. This turns away angry ghosts or other malevolent spirits. The willow branch is held as a healing implement by the benevolent goddess Kwan Yin.

Here is a traditional invocation to call upon Kwan Yin. Throughout the year as well as on Tomb Sweeping Day, it is said that she is infinitely compassionate and will always help whenever there is need, never turning her back on the living or the dead.

Homage to Kwan Yin
  who holds the willow branch,
Homage to the vase hand
  of Kwan Yin.
Bodhisattva of mercy
  whose right hand heals.
She drives away illness.
Her left hand holds the vase
  from which streams the nectar
  of wisdom and compassion.
May it be sprinkled on me,
  all merciful and divine mother
  from the East.

— MARINA BRYONY

Green Tea and Qingming Poetry

Celebrating Tomb Sweeping Day

IN THE CHINESE culture, the annual honoring of one's ancestors marks a time of celebration, as well as obligation. A series of elaborate functions is observed each year near the Spring Equinox. Gravesites are venerated during the ten days before and after Qingming or Tomb Sweeping Day.

Qingming is a movable feast, falling on the 15th day following the Spring Equinox. It's often celebrated on the weekend closest to the actual date to accommodate modern schedules. Feng Shui consultants encourage their clients to make certain that the graves of loved ones are well cared for in order to protect the good fortune of the living.

The Tomb Sweeping holiday is also important in the elaborate and mystical culture surrounding green tea. The quality of tea is determined by the dates when the leaves are picked. The very best and most prestigious tea, commanding the highest price, is gathered early, before Qingming.

Qingming is a popular and recurring theme in art and literature. The famous 12th century painted Qingming Scroll by artist Zhang Zeduan (1085 – 1145) portrays Tomb Sweeping Day festivals during the Song Dynasty. Another example is the Vietnamese epic poem, *The Tale of Kieu*. Some of the most beloved quotes in Vietnamese literature derive from his encounter with the restless ghost during the holiday.

This excerpt from the poem describes scenes from the celebration. It offers some insight into the paradox of Tomb Sweeping Day, a sad holiday which is celebrated joyfully.

*A drizzling rain falls on
The Mourning Day;*

*The mourner's heart is
breaking on his way.*

*Enquiring where can a
wine house be found?*

*A cowherd points to Apricot Flower
Village in the distance.*

*Swift swallows and
spring days were shuttling by;*

*Of ninety radiant ones
three score had fled.*

*Young grass spread all its green
to heaven's rim;*

*Some blossoms marked
pear branches with white dots.*

*Now came the feast of light
in the third month.*

*With graveyard rites and
junkets on the green.*

*As merry pilgrims flocked
from near and far.*

*The sisters and their brother
went for a stroll.*

– GRANIA LING

The Winter Circle

❋ Capella

❋ Pollux

❋ Aldebaran

❋ Procyon   ❋ Betelgeuse

❋ Rigel

❋ Sirius

ON A CLEAR NIGHT in early February between seven and nine PM, look to the southeast for one of the heaven's most memorable sights – the Winter Circle. Seven stars of the first magnitude coil in and around the constellation of Orion.

The three stars in a row that form the Hunter's belt point directly to Sirius, the brightest star in our sky. The ring goes clockwise to Procyon, due north to Pollux, Capella is at 12 o'clock high, Aldebaran at 3, Rigel at 5, and spirals in to end with Betelgeuse, the left shoulder of Orion.

Sirius
The Latin name comes from the Greek word meaning "scorcher," but is commonly known as the Dog Star from its place in Canis Major, Big Dog. This is the Star of Isis known as Sothis to the ancient Egyptians. It is brilliant, bluish, and the first star you'll see after nightfall.

Procyon
A yellow-white star of Canis Minor, Little Dog, is named from the Greek phrase "before the dog" because it rises just before Sirius.

Pollux
Castor and Pollux are the legendary twins of Gemini. Pollux, the brighter of the two, is yellow.

Capella
The "kid" or "little goat" in Latin is the bright yellow eye of Auriga, the Charioteer.

Aldebaran
The orange-red eyes of Taurus, the Bull. Its Arabic name means "the follower" and refers to the star's relation to the cluster of starlets known as the Pleiades, which forms the Bull's hump.

Rigel
The brightest star in Orion is blue-white and represents the Hunter's right foot. Rigel means "foot" in Arabic.

Betelgeuse
"Shoulder of the giant" in Arabic and the red star delineating the left shoulder of Orion, the Hunter. Betelgeuse is the second brightest star in the constellation often called "Winter's Centerpiece."

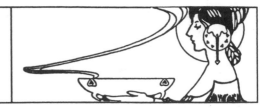

Turmeric

RECENTLY I WAS afflicted with a debilitating sore throat. The pain was so intense I couldn't even swallow my own saliva. Standard over-the-counter remedies — from menthol throat drops to topical analgesic spray — offered little to no relief. My mind began to mull possible diagnoses. Was it strep? Something worse? *Could it be rabies?!* As I scanned my memories for any recent unexplained animal bites, I managed to unearth a forgotten home remedy often employed by my mother: turmeric and honey. Blended into a paste and sucked off a spoon, the sticky honey helps the turmeric coat the throat, offering immediate and sustained respite from pain. The only side-effect I noticed was a bright yellow tongue, stained by turmeric's powerful golden pigment. Who knew relief would come not from the medicine cabinet, but from the pantry? The Ancients, of course!

The distinction between medicine and food is only a modern conceit. Hippocrates famously said, "Let food be your medicine," but the practitioners of Ayurvedic medicine were advocating the same idea thousands of years earlier. Ayurvedic traditions advocate a balanced diet as the best means of achieving a healthy body, mind and spirit. Turmeric, native to the Indian subcontinent, is perhaps the most highly prized tool in their edible arsenal.

One need only look at the names by which turmeric is identified to understand its venerated status. Common names for turmeric include Haridra the Golden One, Gauri the One Whose Face Shines and Kanchani the Golden Goddess. The herb is strongly associated with several of the most powerful deities in the wide Hindu pantheon, such as Vishnu. Turmeric is believed to be a physical manifestation of Shakti, a gift from the feminine creative energy which permeates the universe. Turmeric is essential in many rituals specific to a woman's life cycle, including ritual bathing at puberty, application to the skin and garments for weddings, calling upon the Goddess Lakshmi, and offering pain relief during childbirth. Turmeric is also applied to the shrouds of the deceased before burial. Unusually, turmeric also has equally strong associations with masculine energy and male deities, most notably Haridra Ganapti, one of the thirty-two aspects of Lord Ganesha. In this form Ganesha appears in robes dyed with turmeric. Even his skin takes on the golden hue of the auspicious spice.

Though ritually important, turmeric is equally valued as a medicine. Ingested, it is believed to bring the Doshas, or elemental energies within the human body, into perfect balance. Turmeric aids in digestion and excretion, acts as an anti-inflammatory and pain reliever and can help regulate blood pressure. Applied externally as a component of topical creams, turmeric can prevent infection and speed healing thanks to its anti-bacterial and anti-fungal properties. Turmeric has been used to treat everything from conjunctivitis and eczema to internal parasites. New research even suggest that one of the active ingredients in turmeric, curcumin, may have a role to play in treating various cancers.

But turmeric is not only a multifaceted medicinal plant with deep spiritual roots, it is also uniquely delicious! Most turmeric consumed in the U.S. is in dried, powdered form and can be consumed raw or incorporated into cooked dishes. Turmeric is the main ingredient in most curry powders, lending its distinct pigment and rich flavor (as well as its preservative properties) to any dish it graces. Turmeric's piquant aroma and slightly bitter taste impart an earthy base to dishes. Its taste has been compared to ginger, a relative of turmeric, but there is really no apt comparison. Turmeric must be tasted to be believed!

Tasty Tropical Turmeric Smoothie

1 ripe banana
½ cup whole milk strained yogurt
   (lower fat varieties can be substituted if desired)
1 cup pineapple juice
1 tablespoon coconut oil (coconut milk or cream of coconut can be substituted)
1 teaspoon turmeric
ground black pepper to taste

Put all ingredients in a blender and blend until smooth. Levels can be adjusted to suit individual preferences. The black pepper and fats from the coconut and yogurt will help in the absorption of turmeric, while the banana and pineapple juice will add sweetness to balance turmeric's spicier, earthier tones. Those craving even more sweetness are encouraged to add honey.

– SHANNON MARKS

139

The Mercurial demon of the alchemic philosophers.
From Giovanni Battista Nazari's *Della Transmutatione Metallica*, Brescia, 1589.

The Princess & the DEMON

IT WAS in the reign of King Rameses, son of the Sun, beloved of Amon, king of the gods. A mighty warrior was Rameses; in the day of battle like to Mentu, god of war; very valorous was he, like the son of the Sky-goddess.

Now his Majesty was in Naharaina, where the great river Euphrates rolls down to the sea. And he received the tribute of the vassal-princes, for he was the conqueror of the nine Archer-tribes, and none could stand before his face when he came forth equipped with all his weapons of war. The princes prostrated themselves before him, bowing their foreheads to the ground, breathing the earth which his feet had trodden. Great and splendid was their tribute: gold, and precious stones of all colours, blue lapis lazuli and the green turquoise sacred to Hathor, goddess of love and joy. And slaves came bearing on their backs sweet-scented woods, perfumed and aromatic, like the trees in the land of the Gods.

The prince of Bekhten came also, and with him his eldest daughter; and he placed her in front of the slaves, for she was the choicest part of his tribute. Very beautiful was she, fair in her limbs, tall and slender as a palm-tree, and the heart of the King turned to her with delight, and he loved her more than anything on earth. He made her the Great Royal Wife, and he gave her a name by which she should be known in the land of Egypt; Neferu-Ra, "Beauty of Ra," was she called, for her beauty was like the shining of the sun. And the name was written in the royal oval, as is the custom of the kings of Egypt and their queens.

141

Then King Rameses returned to Egypt, and with him went the Great Royal Wife, Queen Neferu-Ra. And when they came to the Black Land, the land of Egypt, she performed all the ceremonies of a queen in the temples of Egypt.

Now it happened that King Rameses was in Thebes the Mighty on the twenty-second of the month Payni. And he went into the temple of Amon, for this was the day of the beautiful festival of the god, when the boats go up and down upon the water with torches and lights, and the Sacred Barque, adorned with gold and painted with glorious colours, is borne aloft, that men may see the figure of Amon-Ra himself within. And Queen Neferu-Ra was with his Majesty, for the Great Royal Wife in Egypt has ever been the worshipper of Amon-Ra, king of the gods.

There came into the temple courtiers of the King to announce the arrival of a messenger from the prince of Bekhten. Loaded was he with gifts for Neferu-Ra, Queen of Egypt, daughter of the prince of Bekhten, and he carried also a message to the King. When he entered the royal presence, he bowed to the earth saying, "Glory to thee, O Sun of the nine Archer-tribes! May we live before thee!" Then he bowed to the earth again and spoke the message that he had brought from the prince of Bekhten to Rameses, King of Egypt:

"I come to thee, O living King, my Lord, on account of Bent-reshy, the little sister of the Great Royal Wife, Neferu-Ra; for there is a malady in all her limbs. Send therefore a learned man that he may see and heal her."

The King turned to his courtiers and said, "Bring hither a scribe of the House of Life, and bring also those who speak the hidden things of the Inner Chamber." And the courtiers hastened and brought them into the presence forthwith, and the King said to them, "I have brought you hither to hear this matter. Tell me then of a man, learned and skilful, to send to the prince of Bekhten."

Then they took counsel among themselves as to a learned and skilful man, and they brought the scribe Tehuti-em-heb before the King, and the King bade

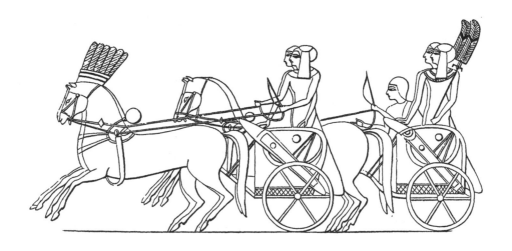

him go with the messenger of the prince of Bekhten to heal Bent-reshy, the little sister of the Great Royal Wife.

When the scribe Tehuti-em-heb came to Bekhten, he was brought into the presence of Bent-reshy. He was a learned and a skilful man, and he found the princess under the dominion of a spirit, a spirit that was hostile to him, against whom his learning and skill were of no avail, who set his magic arts at naught.

Then the prince of Bekhten was sad, and sorrow was in his heart, but Tehuti-em-heb the scribe counselled him to send again to Egypt and to implore the help of Khonsu, the Expeller of Demons, to cast out the evil spirit from Bent-reshy, the little sister of the Great Royal Wife.

Now so great was the distance from Bekhten to Egypt that from the time that Tehuti-em-heb the scribe departed out of Thebes till the second message came to King Rameses was three years, and throughout that time the evil spirit dwelt in Bent-reshy and would not be cast out.

And when the second messenger arrived, King Rameses was again in Thebes, and it was the first of the month Pakhons, the month that is sacred to Khonsu. He entered into the temple, and with him came his courtiers, and the messenger of the prince of Bekhten. In the temple were two statues of Khonsu; very marvellous figures were these, very sacred, very holy; the one was called Khonsu in Thebes Neferhotep, and the other Khonsu, the Expeller of Demons. Now Khonsu is the God of the Moon, the son of Amon-Ra and of Mut,

Lady of Ashru, and men represent him with the curled lock of youth, for he is ever young and beautiful.

Then the King stood before the great statue of Khonsu in Thebes Neferhotep and said, "O my good Lord, I come again into thy presence on account of the daughter of the prince of Bekhten."

Then the priests lifted the statue of Khonsu in Thebes Neferhotep and placed it in front of Khonsu, the Expeller of Demons. And the King spoke again before Khonsu in Thebes Neferhotep and said, "My good Lord, turn thy face to Khonsu, the Expeller of Demons. Grant that he may go to Bekhten."

Khonsu in Thebes Neferhotep inclined his head twice in token of assent. Very marvellous was the figure of Khonsu in Thebes Neferhotep.

And yet again King Rameses spoke, "Let thy protection be with him. Grant that I may send the Majesty of Khonsu to Bekhten to save Bent-reshy, the little sister of the Great Royal Wife."

Khonsu in Thebes Neferhotep inclined his head twice in token of assent. Very marvelous was the figure of Khonsu in Thebes Neferhotep. And he gave his magical protection four times to Khonsu, the Expeller of Demons.

Then King Rameses gave command, and Khonsu, the Expeller of Demons, was placed in the Great Boat; and around the Great Boat were five small boats, with chariots and horses, numerous and splendid, on the right hand and on the left. The retinue of Khonsu, the Expeller of Demons, was the retinue of a king. For a year and five months they journeyed until they reached Bekhten.

The prince of Bekhten came out with his bowmen and his courtiers to meet Khonsu, the Expeller of Demons, with a royal welcome, and they entered into his presence as into the presence of a king. The prince of Bekhten fell on his knees and laid his forehead on the ground at the feet of Khonsu, the Expeller of Demons, and said, "Thou hast come to us. O, be kind to us according to the words of Rameses, King of Egypt."

They brought Khonsu, the Expeller of Demons, to the chamber of Bent-reshy, the little sister of the Great Royal Wife; and he made a magical protection over her. Lo, there happened a wonder and a marvel, for she was well and whole in a moment.

Then the spirit, who had been in her, spoke in the presence of Khonsu, the Expeller of Demons, "Thou hast come in peace, O great God, Expeller of Demons. Bekhten is thy city, its people are thy slaves. I bow before thee, for I also am thy slave. I will go to that place from which I came that thy heart may have peace. But ere I go, let the Majesty of Khonsu give command that a holy day be made for me by the prince of Bekhten."

When he had heard these words, Khonsu, the Expeller of Demons, inclined his head to the priest and said, "Let the prince of Bekhten make a great sacrifice for this spirit."

The prince of Bekhten, and his soldiers and his courtiers heard the voices of the spirit and of the god, and they trembled and were exceedingly afraid. They obeyed the command of the god and prepared a great sacrifice for Khonsu, the Expeller of Demons, and for the spirit that came out of Bent-reshy, the little sister of the Great Royal Wife, the daughter of the prince of Bekhten. And they made a holy day with offerings, sacrifices, and libations.

So the spirit, in the form of a Shining One, went his way in peace out of the land of Bekhten, and he went whithersoever it pleased him, as Khonsu, the Expeller of Demons, had commanded.

The prince of Bekhten was glad and his heart rejoiced, and all the people rejoiced also that the spirit had been driven out of Bent-reshy and out of the land of Bekhten. But in the midst of his joy and gladness, fear came upon the heart of the prince of Bekhten lest the spirit should return and take up his abode again in the land, when Khonsu, the Expeller of Demons, had departed. He took counsel with himself and said, "I will keep Khonsu, the Expeller of Demons, in Bekhten. I will not let him return to Egypt." So Khonsu, the Expeller of Demons, remained three years, four months, and five days in Bekhten, for the prince of Bekhten would not let him go.

And at the end of that time the prince of Bekhten lay upon his bed at night and slept, and while he slept a vision passed before his eyes. He dreamed that he stood before the shrine of Khonsu, the Expeller of Demons; the great doors of the shrine were folded back and the god came forth, stepping out between the doors. He changed into the form of a hawk with feathers of gold, burnished and beautiful, and soared high into the air with wings outspread, and like an arrow he darted towards Egypt.

When the prince of Bekhten awoke, he was exceedingly afraid, for he feared the wrath of the Gods. And he sent for the priest of Khonsu, the Expeller of Demons, and said to him, "The god is estranged from us, he has returned to Egypt. Let his chariot also return to Egypt." The prince of Bekhten gave command that the god should be taken back to Egypt, and he loaded the god with gifts. Great and numerous were the gifts of all manner of beautiful things that the prince of Bekhten gave to Khonsu, the Expeller of Demons.

For many months they journeyed, and with them went an escort of soldiers and horses from the land of Bekhten. They arrived in safety at Thebes, and entered into the temple of Khonsu in Thebes Neferhotep.

Then Khonsu, the Expeller of Demons, gave to Khonsu in Thebes Neferhotep all the gifts, the rich and costly gifts, which he had received from the prince of Bekhten; nothing did he keep for himself. Thus ended the journey of Khonsu, the Expeller of Demons, the great God.

– MARGARET A. MURRAY

This is an excerpt from Ancient Egyptian Legends *by Margaret A. Murray 1913.*

Located with the large Precinct of Amun-Re at Karnak, in Luxor, Egypt, the Temple of Khonsu is an example of an almost complete New Kingdom temple, and was originally constructed by Ramesses III, on the site of an earlier temple. The gateway of this temple is at the end of the avenue of syphinxes that ran to the Luxor Temple.

– A. Rosengarten, W. Collett-Sandars *A Handbook of Architectural Styles* (New York, NY: Charles Scribner's Sons, 1895)

Weather Lore

January

If grass grows in January, it will grow badly the whole year.

February

When the cat in February lies in the sun,
she will again creep behind the stove in March.

When the north wind does not blow in February,
it will surely come in March.

For every thunder with rain in February,
there will be a cold spell in May.

March

If March comes in with adder's head,
it goes out with peacock's tail.

A bushel of March dust is worth a king's ransom.

A windy March and a rainy April make a beautiful May.

March comes in like a lion and goes out like a lamb.

April

April showers bring May flowers.

A cold, moist April fills the cellar and fattens the cow.

May

Dry May brings nothing.

A May flood never did good.

A swarm of bees in May is worth a load of hay;
a swarm of bees in June is worth a silver spoon;
but a swarm of bees in July is not worth a fly.

June

A dripping June sets all things in tune.

July

If the first of July be rainy weather,
'twill rain more or less for three weeks together.

August

When it rains in August, it rains honey and wine.

September

Fair on the first of September, fair the entire month.

October

Warm October, cold February.

November

If the ice in November will bear a duck,
nothing thereafter but sleet and muck.

December

A warm Christmas, a cold Easter.

As the day lengthens, so the cold strengthens.

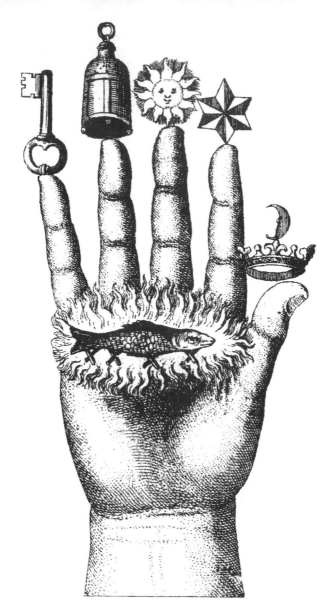

THIS IS THE **Hand of the Philosophers** with their dear secret signs, with which the old sages united with each other and took secret oaths. Nobody can understand this hand with its secret signs, unless he becomes first a juror of the philosophers, (one who swore loyalty to a philosopher), and has loyally served them in the Art Alchemia. Consequently, those who have not this Hand and do not understand its secret signs, nor have taken the oath of loyalty, are bastards in this Art. They do not possess the philosophers' treasure.

– Johan Isaac Hollandus
The Hand of the Philosophers With Its Secret Signs –
Heresy in the Roman Catholic Church: A History

Sidonia von Bork, Sorceress

"AMONGST ALL the trials for witchcraft with which we are acquainted, few have attained so great a celebrity as that of the Lady Canoness of Pomerania, Sidonia von Bork."

So begins the preface to *Sidonia von Bork, Die Klosterhexe*, a novel whose title is usually translated as Sidonia the Sorceress, but which literally means Sidonia von Bork, the Monastery Witch.

Sidonia von Bork (also written as von Borcke), the title character, was actually a real person, a Pomeranian noblewoman who lived between 1548 and 1620. Born into a wealthy family, she entered a convent for unmarried noblewomen in 1564. When a dispute between von Bork and the sub-prioress broke out during a mass, both women were arrested. The sub-prioress accused von Bork of witchcraft, stating that von Bork had forced a fortune-teller to ask the devil about her future.

Under torture, the fortune-teller admitted her guilt and accused von Bork and two other women of witchcraft. Eventually, von Bork was charged with murdering six people and causing a noblewoman to be paralyzed, in addition to various charges of consultation with soothsayers, knowing future events, praying the "Judas psalm," and crossing brooms beneath a kitchen table. The total number of charges brought against her were seventy-two.

The "Judas Psalm" (Psalm 109), also called

"A Cry for Vengeance," is the plea of a man to God for justice against someone who has slandered him. He asks God, "Let his days be few... let his children be fatherless, and let his wife be a widow... Let his posterity be cut off, and in the generation following let their name be blotted out."

This alleged recitation of the "Judas Psalm" most likely inspired the novel, whose full English title is *Sidonia the Sorceress: The Supposed Destroyer of the Whole Reigning Ducal House of Pomerania*. Written by Wilhelm Meinhold in 1848, this piece of fiction paints her as a femme fatale and destroyer of families. In the second sentence of the preface, Meinhold says, "She was accused of having by her sorceries caused sterility in many families, particularly in that of the ancient reigning house of Pomerania, and also of having destroyed the noblest scions of that house by an early and premature death." Though von Bork's defense held that the "murder" victims most likely died natural deaths, she was still convicted.

Under torture, Sidonia confessed to witchcraft. She later recanted, only to be tortured again. In 1620, she was beheaded and her body burned outside the mill gate at Stettin, Germany, although the exact date of her death is unknown.

– MORVEN WESTFIELD

⇒ Breathe Easy ⇐

NO MATTER how you look at it, breath is life. From the technical explanations of the taking of air into the lungs and the expelling of air from the lungs to the more esoteric 'power' of breath, breathing is necessary for each and every being. Breath allows us to form sounds and to vocalize, to oxygenate our blood and cells and to cleanse and purify, to a certain degree, our systems upon exhalation. Breath also allows us to focus and still our minds and bodies. Focused breathing sharpens our intentions and strengthens connections to ourselves, our environment and to those within it. By focusing on the physical processes and growing awareness occurring within, the keys to expansiveness and consciousness can be found and the locks turned; thresholds uncovered by opening doors. Learning to gather, train and manipulate our breath and its focus is pivotal to not only exerting intentional influence on our lives, both secular and sacred. It is the fulcrum for balance within.

In the mundane, the physical explanation of breath is straightforward. Air from our environment is inhaled through the mouth or nose, travels into the lungs and is exhaled out of the body and back into our environment. Our bodies do this without much conscious thought, thousands of times throughout each day and night. Yet even this 'simple' action is much more than oxygen in and carbon dioxide out; more than the tensing and the relaxing of muscles, of the mechanical process of respiration. If we link this process with memory and the mindful observance and training of breath, how much more focused and abundant does our mundane life become? How much richer, how much more expansive does our spiritual life and personal practice become? What happens when the two are combined? Just as there are environmental particles hitching a ride upon the inhalation current flowing into our bodies and the various types of waste and 'goo' flowing out of our bodies upon exhalation, the same clutter of particles and outside influences can be found in our mind, within our spirit and our energies; blocking or delaying growth, awareness and connections.

"I am here, in the now."

While reflecting upon possible benefits of bringing conscious breath to our everyday mundane lives, focus and clarity in decision making stand out as two truly valuable advantages. Emotions, be they our own or streaming from those around us, can be a challenge in our daily lives whether we encounter them within the professional or personal arena. Conscious breath allows us to detach from the flooding core emotions, enabling a more objective, rather than subjective, view of a given situation. By keeping the extraneous bits of the experience outside of ourselves while bringing our own inner awareness to bear as a sort of filter, clarity and letting go become easier and the build-up of the many experiences we carry when we need not may be reduced.

"I am here, in the now." Being present in the now, rather than allowing one's mind to wander into the past or future, is absolute zero in this equation. Breath can be utilized to get one into the 'zone' quickly and efficiently. Conscious use of breath can clear the mind, slow the heart rate, dissipate excess emotion and direct the flow of thought and energy. Breath connects our mind with our own innate power center, our gut intuition and knowing. This awareness also brings recognition of personal substance, the knowledge of occupying space and volume, further grounding us in the now, enabling us to evaluate, formulate and implement decisions and plans. Breath gives power and focus to our intent. While focusing and funneling our intent, breath also powers that which we do not observe with mundane senses. How does one harness and train this breath 'muscle memory'?

Meditation

Meditation is one way in which a person may utilize intentional breath and breathing. An integral component of many spiritual practices, meditation is a way of training the brain to tune into different levels of consciousness and can help establish and foster a beneficial connection between mind, body and spirit. It is a practice of mindfulness which can be used to observe, without judgment, one's own beliefs, actions and feelings. What is mindfulness? Mindfulness is a non-judgmental awareness and is constantly open and evolving — a fluid state of being and observation. It is an active focus on the now, the moment one is experiencing, allowing an openness and being which naturally weaves through and around the fluid tapestry of meditation.

There are many types and avenues by which to explore this practice. For example, moving meditation such as Tai Chi, guided meditation in which a person (or group of people) is 'led' by another practitioner reading or verbally prompting visualization journeys or situations, or self- guided meditation where the practitioner attains alpha states via music, internal dialogue or well-worn visualization methods. Whether one employs one of the many meditation methods, or simply ventures out into nature with mind and senses open and observant, breath control is the key to successful meditation.

Clear vision

Any successful manifestation requires a clear vision. Whether this creation is accomplished with visual clues such as photographs, vision boards or by constructing and expanding upon a well-honed internal vision, the foundation must be a clearly defined concept. Too often we are pulled in many different directions or have lost our focus and connection with what it is that we truly wish to accomplish. Every interaction with others imparts viable and useful information as well as unnecessary 'fluff' some of which does not roll off of our backs as easily as we might think.

The ability and practice of controlling our breath can be advantageous in any situation. Thinking about changing careers or jobs? Fallen out of love, or even like, with your current position, coworkers or company? Relationship in turmoil? Familial bonds being tested or broken? The thoughts of change alone can be overwhelming. Emotion, guilt, duty, daily demands and dependent responsibilities seem to compete for rapidly fleeting and increasingly finite reasoning ability.

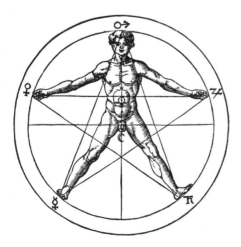

Focusing on each individual breath, track the intake of air, following its path through the head and body, pushing the energy along the veins and meridians. Visualizing existing pathways and flow within and around us can bring us back in touch with a place of discernment and clarity. A place where one step, one piece of the puzzle can be observed, shined up and adjusted or released. Trade the sand through your fingers for the solidity of now using breath.

Quiet mind

Breath training and practice can benefit spiritual development as well. Desiring to delve a bit deeper in your spirituality? Feeling a tug or a call? The quieter the mind, the more accurately we may ascertain to whom or where we are being led — the more open our awareness welcomes what comes. Want to develop a deeper connection to the divine? Has an alternative healing modality, such as Reiki or Polarity, caught your interest? Want to strengthen your energy manipulation and movement skills? Focused breath uses will as fuel and direction for your purpose, be it healing or working. Aspire to connect with another person, Spirit or group on a deeper level? It is a special and absolutely sacred experience to breathe, feel and share that force of life with another, with trusted others.

A simple exercise to bring awareness to breath and breathing is to sit or lie on a comfortable surface, close the eyes and inhale through the nose for a count of eight. Feel the air and the action of the diaphragm during this process. Hold this breath for a count of eight and then exhale for a count of eight through the mouth. This simple technique grounds and connects to the now, and can be used in conjunction with mind-clearing exercises (visualizing a blank TV screen and erasing random thoughts and 'noise' using breath, for example), body relaxing exercises (i.e. starting at the toes, point and flex each muscle group while directing attention and breath to the area being worked upon ending with the head), or for chakra alignment exercises (beginning at the root or between the feet depending upon personal preference). There are many varied practices both mundane and spiritual which may be enhanced by developing a routine of conscious breath.

Breathing properly and with intention can reduce anxiety, clear the mind, relax the physical body and forge a deeper awareness of the body, mind and spirit. Controlled breath and breathing have been used by many cultures, some for centuries. Once a level of competency with the basics has been established, other modalities such as acupressure, energy techniques, chakra workings, herbal practices and potions, space clearing, ancestor communication, advanced meditation and psychic development techniques may be added to and expanded upon. Breathing practices may be honed with groups or individually — the limits only as solid as the strictures of the mind and the willingness of the practitioner.

– TAMMI WILSON

153

the fixed stars

Zaniah

4 Degrees 31 minutes of Libra

IN A STATELY dance, innumerable stars drift ever so slowly across the night sky, sparkling in the sphere of space which holds our zodiac. Called the fixed stars, they were named by stargazers long ago to distinguish them from the rapidly moving planets which twirl around the Sun. Over 72 years a fixed star will move a single degree. Members of distant galaxies, they pulsate with an energy field unique to each. The fixed stars hold vast stores of important information, bringing messages for good or evil. These might be compared to important footnotes when added to the interpretation of the planets in an astrology chart. Use an orb of just 3 degrees when considering the importance of a fixed star in a horoscope.

The mythology behind the constellations, which are outlines formed by the fixed stars, offer specific information about their influences. Since 2006 *The Witches' Almanac* has featured a different fixed star each year. This year our choice is Zaniah, currently positioned at 4 degrees 31 minutes of Libra. Zaniah is a variable star which twinkles on the southern wing of Virgo. Its name translates as an angle or

corner in the Kennel of the Barking Dogs. The writings of Ptolemy and Alvidas are extremely favorable regarding the influence of Zaniah. Both of these legendary astrologers attribute Zaniah with all of the best qualities of Mercury and Venus. Refinement, true love, honor, eloquence, poetry and a kindly nature are its keynotes.

During the year to come, the lunar eclipse on March 23, 2016, at 3 degrees Libra will conjoin Zaniah, emphasizing its benevolent potential in world affairs, as well as in the lives of individuals. When Jupiter, the most fortunate of planets, enters Libra in 2016 it will be within orb of a conjunction with Zaniah September 14 – October 16. Overall, a positive cycle can be expected then. Those with planets or house cusps near 4 degrees of Libra in their birth charts will feel the most benefit.

People born September 24 – 30 of any year will have the Sun in conjunction with Zaniah. Additionally, check your own horoscope for placements from 1 to 7 degrees of Libra to determine whether Zaniah impacts you.

– DIKKI-JO MULLEN

The Interpretation of Zaniah in the Birth Chart

With the Sun
Studious, educated, popular, sociable, happy marriage

With the Moon
Very concerned for others, can be overly sympathetic and charitable, involved in legal matters

With Mercury
Musical and artistic gifts, good writer, wide social circle

With Venus
A quick learner, talent in the fine arts (especially music), many friends, considerable wealth

With Mars
Athletic, assertive, a chaotic romantic life, should avoid legal entanglements

With Jupiter
Philosophical mind, deep religious faith, respect from others, many journeys

With Saturn
Solemn, hard working, gains through older people or an inheritance

With Uranus
Excellent psychic ability, creative, prefers a calm life, supportive friends

With Neptune
Kindly, can attract odd relationships and eccentric associates, helpful acquaintances, favorable marriage

With Pluto
All is sacrificed for love, scandal regarding a questionable love situation, must heed rules

With the Part of Fortune
Excellent sales and promotional skills bring opportunities

With the Ascendant
A pleasing appearance creates good first impressions, creates a comfortable environment, loves luxury

Moon Cycles

A New Moon rises with the Sun,
Her waxing half at midday shows,
The Full Moon climbs at sunset hour,
And waning half the midnight knows.

NEW	2017	FULL	NEW	2018	FULL
January 27		January 12	January 16		January 1, 31*
February 26		February 10	February 15		No full moon
March 27		March 12	March 17		March 1, 31*
April 26		April 11	April 15		April 29
May 25		May 10	May 15		May 29
June 23		June 9	June 13		June 28
July 23		July 9	July 12		July 27
August 21		August 7	August 11		August 26
September 20		September 6	September 9		September 24
October 19		October 5	October 8		October 24
November 18		November 4	November 7		November 23
December 18		December 3	December 7		December 22

* Blue Moons on January 31, 2018 and March 31, 2018

Life takes on added dimension when you match your activities to the waxing and waning of the Moon. Observe the sequence of her phases to learn the wisdom of constant change within complete certainty.

Dates are for Eastern Standard and Daylight Time.

presage

by Dikki-Jo Mullen

ARIES 2016 – PISCES 2017

THE SPRINGTIME marks a new zodiacal cycle. Fresh adventures and dreams are guided by consulting astrology, the language of the stars. The celestial patterns can reveal all that is important to know in order to brighten the personal journey during the times ahead.

Jupiter, the largest of planets, is in Virgo from the Vernal Equinox until September 9. Jupiter expands, and the sign of Virgo closely links to maintaining the most precious of treasures, that of good health. Natural and preventative health care has long appealed to those who follow the craft. This year in the health sections of Presage you will find suggestions regarding the cell salts that correlate to each sign of the zodiac. Cell salts are naturally occurring minerals in a highly purified form. They are found in foods but can also be purchased as capsules.

Saturn in Sagittarius trines Uranus in Aries all year. This is a bright, fiery and progressive pattern. It encourages new lifestyle choices for many. Attitudes about survival and priorities are moving in a new direction. Flexibility and a willingness to grow will assure success now.

This year brings six eclipses; two will be in Pisces, and one each in Libra, Aquarius, Virgo and Leo. Spiritual beliefs, the law, partnerships and marriage, politics, charity, the entertainment world and health care are all subject to significant changes.

To explore what this will mean in your own life, first read the Presage segment for your Sun sign. This shows where your life force and energy are focused, literally where you will shine. Next consider the section describing your Moon sign to understand how your emotional needs can be met. Finally, study the segment for your ascendant, which concerns the reputation and how others perceive you.

ASTROLOGICAL KEYS

Signs of the Zodiac
Channels of Expression

ARIES: fiery, pioneering, competitive
TAURUS: earthy, stable, practical
GEMINI: dual, lively, versatile
CANCER: protective, traditional
LEO: dramatic, flamboyant, warm
VIRGO: conscientious, analytical
LIBRA: refined, fair, sociable
SCORPIO: intense, secretive, ambitious
SAGITTARIUS: friendly, expansive
CAPRICORN: cautious, materialistic
AQUARIUS: inquisitive, unpredictable
PISCES: responsive, dependent, fanciful

Elements
FIRE: Aries, Leo, Sagittarius
EARTH: Taurus, Virgo, Capricorn
AIR: Gemini, Libra, Aquarius
WATER: Cancer, Scorpio, Pisces

Qualities

CARDINAL	FIXED	MUTABLE
Aries	Taurus	Gemini
Cancer	Leo	Virgo
Libra	Scorpio	Sagittarius
Capricorn	Aquarius	Pisces

CARDINAL signs mark the beginning of each new season — active.
FIXED signs represent the season at its height — steadfast.
MUTABLE signs herald a change of season — variable.

Celestial Bodies
Generating Energy of the Cosmos

Sun: birth sign, ego, identity
Moon: emotions, memories, personality
Mercury: communication, intellect, skills
Venus: love, pleasures, the fine arts
Mars: energy, challenges, sports
Jupiter: expansion, religion, happiness
Saturn: responsibility, maturity, realities
Uranus: originality, science, progress
Neptune: dreams, illusions, inspiration
Pluto: rebirth, renewal, resources

Glossary of Aspects

Conjunction: two planets within the same sign or less than 10 degrees apart, favorable or unfavorable according to the nature of the planets.

Sextile: a pleasant, harmonious aspect occurring when two planets are two signs or 60 degrees apart.

Square: a major negative effect resulting when planets are three signs from one another or 90 degrees apart.

Trine: planets four signs or 120 degrees apart, forming a positive and favorable influence.

Quincunx: a mildly negative aspect produced when planets are five signs or 150 degrees apart.

Opposition: a six sign or 180° separation of planets generating positive or negative forces depending on the planets involved.

The Houses — *Twelve Areas of Life*

1st house: appearance, image, identity
2nd house: money, possessions, tools
3rd house: communications, siblings
4th house: family, domesticity, security
5th house: romance, creativity, children
6th house: daily routine, service, health
7th house: marriage, partnerships, union
8th house: passion, death, rebirth, soul
9th house: travel, philosophy, education
10th house: fame, achievement, mastery
11th house: goals, friends, high hopes
12th house: sacrifice, solitude, privacy

Eclipses

Eclipses bring about turning points, shifts, growth and surprises. For those with a birthday within three days of an eclipse can expect a year of breakthroughs and important changes. There will be six partial eclipses this year.

March 23, 2016	Full Moon lunar eclipse in Libra, north node
August 18, 2016	Full Moon lunar eclipse in Aquarius, south node
September 1, 2016	New Moon solar eclipse in Virgo, north node
September 16, 2016	Full Moon lunar eclipse in Pisces, south node
February 10, 2017	Full Moon lunar eclipse in Leo, north node
February 26, 2017	New Moon solar eclipse in Pisces, south node

A total eclipse is more influential than a partial. Eclipses conjunct the Moon's north node are thought to be more favorable than those which conjoin the south node.

Retrograde Planetary Motion

Retrogrades, being quite significant, promise a change of pace and perspective.

Mercury Retrograde

Retrograde Mercury impacts technology, travel, and communication. Those who have been out of touch return. Complete old projects, revise, review and tread familiar paths. Gemini and Virgo will be affected.

April 28 – May 22, 2016 in Taurus
August 30 – Sept. 22, 2016 in Virgo
Dec. 19, 2016 – Jan. 8, 2017
in Capricorn and Sagittarius

Venus Retrograde

Venus retrograde influences art, love and finances. Taurus and Libra will be affected.

March 4 – April 15, 2017
in Aries and Pisces

Mars Retrograde

The military, sports and heavy industry are impacted. Aries and Scorpio will be affected.

April 17 – June 29, 2016
in Sagittarius and Scorpio

Jupiter Retrograde

Large animals, speculation, education and religion are impacted. Sagittarius and Pisces are affected.

January 8 – May 9, 2016 in Virgo
Feb. 6 – June 9, 2017 in Libra

Saturn Retrograde

Elderly people, the disadvantaged, employment and natural resources are linked to Saturn. Capricorn and Aquarius will be affected.

March 25 – Aug. 13, 2016 in Sagittarius

Uranus Retrograde

Inventions, science, revolutionaries and extreme weather relate to Uranus retrograde. Aquarius is impacted.

July 29 – December 29, 2016 in Aries

Neptune Retrograde

Water, aquatic creatures, chemicals, spiritual forces and psychic phenomena are impacted by Neptune retrograde. Pisces will be affected.

June 13 – November 19, 2016 in Pisces

Pluto Retrograde

Ecology, espionage, birth and death rates, nuclear power and mysteries relate to Pluto retrograde. Scorpio will be affected.

April 18 – Sept. 26, 2016 in Capricorn

ARIES

March 20 – April 19

Spring 2016 – Spring 2017 for those
born under the sign of the Ram

Always courageous and energetic, the Ram acts with confidence. Challenges present greater inspiration to succeed. Because you are a leader and pioneer, uncharted territory of any kind beckons to you. You relish releasing the past, experimenting with a fresh outlook, and starting over.

March 22 – April 5 Mercury transits Aries while racing hand in hand with the Sun. The pace is quick and interesting. You'll communicate exceptionally well, winning over the hearts and minds of others with your eloquence. On April 7, at the New Moon in Aries, a wonderful four-week cycle for love and creativity commences. Social connections are promising. Great happiness comes your way by May Eve.

During May and June Mars, your ruler, will be retrograde. Expect delays. Be patient if a project takes longer than expected. Past life connections and reunions of all kinds will be a focus. Pace yourself regarding strenuous activities. Rest for both mind and body can rejuvenate you. Celebrate a quiet Summer Solstice peacefully at home.

Early July brings a surprise regarding your family. A relative might announce a move or new career plans.

A peek at your genealogy offers intriguing perspectives concerning ancestors. July 13 – August 5 finds Venus brightening your sector of leisure and romance. Honor the deepest stirrings of your heart by expressing true love at Lammastide. Favorable aspects between the Sun, Saturn and Uranus in fire signs bring a sense of ease and accomplishment during August. Pressure lessens. A goal is reached. Take a vacation, and appreciate summer sports.

September 1 brings an eclipse in your 6th house of health. Transits of the Sun and retrograde Mercury will follow through the Autumnal Equinox. Maintaining health and fitness is at the forefront in your life. This can involve your personal health, the well-being of a loved one or a cherished animal companion. Remain vigilant and well informed. Address any health concerns and all will be well.

As September ends, a coworker might have a personal situation arise which impacts your daily schedule. Be flexible and adapt to changes. October brings strong aspects involving Mars and Pluto in your 10th house. You'll sense undercurrents and competition regarding professional aspirations and status. The Full Moon in Aries on October 16 sheds light on your role in this. Research new developments in your field, especially regarding science and technology.

All Hallows arrives with a lovely, upbeat trine from Venus, lasting until mid-November. Watch a Halloween genre film or attend a guided ghost tour. How about a travel-oriented costume choice? November 13 – December 1 Mercury joins Saturn in your 9th house. Long distance travel, an interesting new field of study or a broader spiritual perception may captivate you. New ideas are presented; your opinions are shifting. December 1 – 19 an interplay between Mars and Uranus focuses on your 11th house. The expectations of friends, community life and your role in an organization can impact your holiday season. At the Winter Solstice burn white candles and sage to bless and release friendships or group affiliations which you have outgrown.

Late December through January 28 promises a strong emphasis on your 12th house. With Neptune involved your dreams can be especially meaningful. Record impressions upon awakening and study the symbolism. Dreams might offer valuable insights concerning impending situations. You will appreciate some solitude and be more reserved than usual during the weeks before Candlemas. Meditation will be appealing. On February 4 Venus joins Uranus in your sign where it will remain through winter's end, bringing a renewed sparkle to your image and appearance. A new hairstyle or choice of apparel can be a part of this Others will see you as unpredictable and charming. February and March favor networking.

HEALTH
The cell salt for Aries is potassium phosphate, K_3PO_4. This cell salt is thought to help treat skin conditions as well as the depression and headaches your birth sign is often prone to. Your cell salt can be found in garlic, bran, dates, mustard greens, peppers and wheat germ.

LOVE
The week of the Vernal Equinox brings a new slant on partnership and commitment issues. This is punctuated by turning points and surprises because the eclipse at the Full Moon on March 23 affects your 7th house of close relationships. Happiness regarding love is indicated during late winter when a very long Venus transit through Aries begins.

SPIRITUALITY
The eclipses on September 16 and February 26 will emphasize your sector of spirituality. Volunteer work and other charitable endeavors can generate meaningful spiritual awakening near those times. An awareness of how everything that happens is connected to the sacrifice of something else is a recurring theme concerning your spiritual path this year.

FINANCE
During the first three weeks of May, Venus will bless your 2nd house of earnings and cash flow. This trend favors financial matters. From September 10 through the end of winter a Jupiter opposition can make you overly generous or vulnerable to faulty advice. Seek bargains regarding major purchases. Hesitate before allowing others to influence your financial decisions from September through March. Heed your own better judgment first.

TAURUS
April 20 – May 20
Spring 2016 – Spring 2017 for those
born under the sign of the Bull

Persevering and practical, you are a dedicated, devoted worker and loyal in love. Security and stability, both emotionally and financially, are always top priorities. You are inclined to plan ahead and can be quite stubborn if others attempt to force you to change once you have selected a direction. Always sensitive to sounds, you enjoy music. Nature's beauty appeals to you too. Taurus is often a gifted landscaper and gardener.

As the springtime begins you'll be doing some sleuthing. Mars transits your 8th house. There is a mystery you are determined to solve. On April 6 Mercury enters your birth sign, a trend which lasts until June 11. Travel plans or an intriguing new course of study present new perspectives. The specifics will be highlighted near the New Moon in your sign on May 6. May is a wonderful time to revisit destinations or pursue projects which have interested you before.

Devote the Summer Solstice to blessing your finances. Reciting prosperity affirmations can be very effective. Select a talisman, perhaps a coin minted in your year of birth, to secure your income. During July, home and family life will be a source of happiness as your 4th house will be highlighted. Home improvements or even the purchase of a new residence can favorably impact your living circumstances. Plan a house blessing at Lammastide. August finds Venus and Jupiter, the celestial benefics, trine your Sun. This promises an especially enjoyable time during the bright, warm summer days. Your creative gifts will shine. A child's accomplishments can also add to your happiness.

The eclipses on September 1 and 16 usher in new long-term goals. Neptune, the planet of dreams and visions, is prominent. Guidance and inspiration can come upon awakening from sleep or following a meditation session. At the Autumnal Equinox Jupiter and the Sun will affect your 6th house. This promises improvement in health and vitality as the new season begins. An exceptional animal companion can enter your life unexpectedly near the New Moon on September 30. Through October 17 your ruler, Venus, will oppose your Sun. Others reach out to you and make well-intentioned plans, but you might feel a bit rushed by their suggestions. Be flexible and receptive and all will be well. Halloween brings a deep and intense mood. A good costume choice might be a private detective or a spy. Consider a Mata Hari look or a favorite figure from a mystery novel.

A strong Mars aspect November 1 – 9 finds you motivated; much can be accomplished. The Full Moon in Taurus on November 16 activates favorable influences in earth signs, with Venus prominent. Make holiday plans. From mid-November through December 7 shopping excursions and social events are fulfilling. Life is good. Career situations are a concern during the remainder of December. A difficult coworker can be a source of concern or stress. At the Winter Solstice construct a small circle of crystals to bless a tense situation at work.

As January begins, the accent is on cooperation and networking. Develop a support system; a friend appreciates your kindness. A favor is returned just before Candlemas. Assume a role of greater leadership within an organization if the opportunity arises. February finds a stellium of planets gathering in your 12th house, a pattern which remains through winter's end. You will cherish a bit of peace and privacy. The inherent magic in secrecy will call to you. It's also a wonderful time to connect with wild animals or to appreciate undeveloped forest land. Charitable projects will be rewarding. Be generous with others and you will receive an unexpected favor or break. Venus, your ruler, turns retrograde at the beginning of March, ushering in a touch of awkwardness. Patience helps. Through the month's end a touch of humor and tolerance will bring out the brightest and best regarding both love and finances.

HEALTH
The cell salt sodium sulfate, Na_2SO_4, is linked to Taurus. Since your birth sign rules the ears and throat, disorders tied to those areas might improve by ingesting this cell salt. It has also been used to treat fluid retention, gallstones, swelling and constipation. Your cell salt can be found in rosemary, celery, chard, spinach and radishes.

LOVE
From the springtime through September 10 Jupiter will transit your 5th house of love and romance. This whole time is promising for developing an important and nurturing love connection. November 12 – December 7 finds your sector of pleasure and romance highlighted by both Venus and Pluto. Love assumes a gentle and sentimental quality. A joyful interlude brings happy memories to cherish for the future.

SPIRITUALITY
The Full Moon on July 19 will conjoin Pluto in Capricorn. This impacts your 9th house of philosophy and higher thought. The practical application of spiritual truths results. Work with sacred stones and herbs to enhance spiritual perceptions. Late winter emphasizes your 12th house. This favors quiet reverie. Heed the small, still voice within. Your hunches offer spiritual insights concerning important lifestyle choices.

FINANCE
A favorable grand trine in earth sign transits April 6 – June 10 promises wonderful financial opportunities. Mercury, ruler of your financial sector, is involved. Consider vocational study to enhance salable job skills. Travel, perhaps for business, can also boost your income. Research current trends in your career field. Exercise careful judgment regarding a risky financial suggestion made by another during July.

GEMINI

May 21 – June 20

Spring 2016 – Spring 2017 for those
born under the sign of the Twins

Adaptable, articulate and exuberant Gemini has a talent for the expression and exchange of ideas. With a spontaneous charm, the bright, versatile and multi-faceted Twins adjust to almost any situation with aplomb. You will abandon a project if it becomes repetitious or weighty. Forever airy and ephemeral you are truly mercurial, thriving on change. You are at your best when you're involved in several projects simultaneously.

The springtime begins with an eclipse in your 5th house of romance and pleasure. Unexpectedly, a new creative project or love interest captivates you. Mercury dashes through your 11th house, playing tag with Uranus through April 5. Your goals are in flux; you are in the mood to explore and experiment. Mid-April through May 27 Mars will oppose your Sun. Competition intensifies, and a partner challenges your ideas. Work to negotiate a mutually acceptable compromise. A legal or ethical matter can be involved.

The New Moon in Gemini on June 6 will conjoin Venus. Tension lessens. Loving support and admiration comes your way from the important people in your life. The remainder of June finds

Mercury in Gemini. You will be especially alert and observant, making the best choices while combining business with pleasure. Observe the Summer Solstice by sharing an anecdote or riddle which includes a cleverly disguised kernel of wisdom.

July begins with an emphasis on finances. Budgeting for a special purchase can be a consideration. Get enough rest during the last half of the month. Mars will ignite your health sector. The pace can get rather hyper. You might be burning the candle at both ends. Lammastide favors a simple and restful observance; make time to rest and regroup. August finds Saturn completing its retrograde in your 7th house of relationships. A close partner assumes new responsibilities or faces an obstacle. Be supportive, but do remember that sometimes there is just so much that can be done for another. Back away from someone who becomes overly demanding.

The eclipses on September 1 and 16 profoundly affect two of your important angular houses, the 4th and 10th. This heralds a new cycle regarding both your residence and family dynamics and public visibility. At the Autumnal Equinox consult the Tarot or tea leaves for more insight into your career situation. Synchronicities arise which may be omens offered by helpful spirit guides and angels. Late September through October 18 brings a beneficial Venus transit in your health sector. Time spent with loved ones and involvement in activities you truly enjoy will enhance wellness. Pleasing music, colors and fragrances used in alternative healing modalities boost well-being too.

As Halloween nears, favorable Mercury and Jupiter aspects promise opportunities for travel and bring invitations to social functions. For your costume this year consider a vagabond, sports or Old West look. November 9 – December 19 a Mars influence encourages the exploration of new ideas. Visit a library or bookstore or enroll in a study program. Be patient if an in-law or grandchild seems a little demanding. Humor and talking over your differences might help. Mercury turns retrograde by the Winter Solstice; this remains in force until January 9. The winter holidays will invoke a nostalgic mood. News arrives concerning those who have been a part of your past.

Throughout January Venus will join Neptune in your 10th house. The support of friends and a series of coincidences will advance your professional status and public image. An inspiring hunch or creative idea can change your professional prospects for the better by Candlemas. February renews your vitality and motivation due to a favorable Mars aspect. Your workload eases, especially February 23 – 28. March 1 – 13 a serious mood will develop due to a strong Saturn aspect. Be cautious about making commitments and promises. There might be more involved than is first apparent.

HEALTH
Your birth sign's cell salt is potassium chloride, KCl. It generally helps form healthy bones and cells, including the arms and hands, which are ruled by Gemini. Your cell salt stimulates better absorption of nutrients by the body as a whole too and has been credited with alleviating malnutrition. Strawberries, parsley, blueberries, pineapple, cucumbers and asparagus are good sources for your cell salt.

LOVE
The eclipse on March 23 can bring a change of status regarding a liaison. From September 10 throughout the winter Jupiter will transit your 5th house of love and pleasure. This promises genuine happiness and great good fortune regarding romantic bliss.

SPIRITUALITY
Focus on Full Moon observances to facilitate spiritual awakening this year. The lunar eclipse on August 18 profoundly affects your sector of higher consciousness. The Full Moon in Gemini on December 13 makes a strong Saturn aspect, suggesting that honoring the passage of time and interactions with those who are of a different generation can provide spiritual perspectives.

FINANCE
Shortly after your birthday a series of favorable transits will affect your financial sector. This peaks at the New Moon on July 4 and continues through July 12. Explore financial opportunities and work on your budget during this time. The Full Moon on January 12 illuminates your financial situation. Meditate at moonrise that night to understand what must be done to assure security throughout the times to come.

CANCER
June 21 – July 22
Spring 2016 – Spring 2017 for those
born under the sign of the Crab

Sensitive to the feelings and moods of others, Cancerians are considerate and responsive. Ruled by the changeable Moon, you're attached to home and family, but will also enjoy travel and variety. Focus your vivid imagination toward positive thoughts and scenarios. Release past disappointments and look forward to the future.

Your household feels unsettled as spring begins. The eclipse on March 23 hints at a move or shift. The specifics will develop throughout the spring. Explore new avenues of creative expression. Mid-April through late May seek ways to release stress. Take routine precautions regarding health and fitness. Both Mars and Saturn will be retrograde in your 6th house. This can impact the wellness of animal companions, your cousins or even aunts and uncles. Dedicate May Eve rites to a health blessing.

During June and July, Mars impacts your pleasure and love sector. This assures a higher energy level by your birthday. Celebrate the Summer Solstice by attending the theater, a concert or visiting an art gallery. June 18 – July 12 Venus glides through Cancer, forming a grand water sign trine with Neptune and Mars. This indicates overall happiness and appreciation from those you care for. Responsibilities will be easier to cope with. Others will be helpful and supportive. Mercury races through your financial sector during the last half of July. Business meetings, travel for professional reasons and new publications offer opportunities to increase your income.

By Lammastide Uranus will be retrograde in your 10th house of status and success. This lasts until December 30. Observe repeating patterns while making career plans. Heed a sense of déjà vu; the past will reveal the future. Elements of the unexpected are afoot. August 1 – 5 favors financial matters, as the Sun and Venus favorably influence your sector of earnings and security.

September brings a T-square aspect and two eclipses in the mutable signs. This affects your state of mind. Your thoughts and words are creating your reality. Repeat positive affirmations and keep an attitude of gratitude. September is an excellent time to learn new things. Consider joining a book club, class or discussion group. At the Autumnal Equinox write a wish list, perhaps illustrated with pictures, to help manifest desirable situations.

October finds the Sun, Mercury and Jupiter in your 4th house. This is wonderful for residential real estate transactions, making home improvements and enjoying family time. The Full Moon on October 16 has you working to balance professional obligations with your home life.

You'll feel nostalgic near Halloween. For your costume, consider a vintage look. Resurrect a hat, suit or gown from your attic or a thrift shop. November 1 – 11 finds Venus and Saturn in your 6th house. Outstanding rapport with animal companions brings joy and healing. Try meditating with a familiar, possibly entering its world for a few moments. Helpful insights regarding your own health also come about in early November.

The last half of November through the Winter Solstice is all about relationships. A legal issue could arise. Several planetary transits highlight your 7th house. A partner might voice important goals and dreams. Others will affect your plans near December 4 – 7.

As winter begins, Mercury is retrograde, a trend which culminates on January 9. Use care regarding promises or signing documents. The terms might be difficult to fulfill, especially if an estate or other legal matter is involved. The Full Moon in Cancer on January 12 is a time to focus on self understanding. Consider the axiom from the Temple of Delphi, "know thyself." Adapt to abrupt changes in the status quo in mid-January.

At Candlemas light a taper to cherish your professional reputation. Mars, Venus and Mercury will all join Uranus in your 10th house while in opposition to Jupiter. Challenging aries. Heed your own better judgment and all will be well. February – March presents an exciting and pivotal time regarding your own long-term fame and fortune.

HEALTH
The cell salt calcium fluoride, CaF, impacts your birth sign. This salt is thought to protect the breast and stomach, which can be vulnerable areas for you. It also stimulates the elasticity of muscles and health of teeth, nails, bones and veins. Cataracts and receding gums have been treated with it as well. Food sources for your cell salt are carrots, cabbage, kale and watercress.

LOVE
Tender-hearted Venus brings promising love prospects your way March 22 to April 5, late June through mid-July, September 24 to October 18, and again January 4 to February 3. Share time strolling the beach, sailing or perhaps river rafting with a loved one. Set a romantic mood by cooking a meal at home together.

SPIRITUALITY
The eclipses on September 16 and February 26 favor your 9th house of spirituality. Find spiritual strength and expansion through maintaining faith and ritual observances. Visiting a sacred site and working with dream interpretation can enhance spirituality. A sea shell or water elemental would be an excellent charm to encourage spirituality.

FINANCE
The Sun rules your 2nd house of finances. Try to finalize important financial transactions at noon, when the Sun is directly overhead. This is especially true on Sundays and Mondays. July 13 – August 22 is promising for profit and gain. The Full Moon on February 10 reveals important details regarding finances and how to plan for security.

LEO

July 23 – August 22

Spring 2016 – Spring 2017 for those
born under the sign of the Lion

Creative and dramatic, Leo's natural
warmth and zest for life makes a natural leader. Dignified and optimistic, you
are tolerant and broad-minded. Others
often perceive you as a role model.
With a touch of showmanship you are
driven to excel and usually refuse to
settle for less than the best.

Springtime begins with powerful
and positive transits in your fellow fire
signs of Sagittarius and Aries. This
highlights your 5th and 9th houses.
Love, adventure, recreation and travel
are the focus through April. Fresh concepts inspire you at the New Moon on
April 7. A benevolent influence involving your career appears when Venus
crosses your midheaven on May Eve.
Expressing creative ideas and networking will bring you recognition during
May. Respect traditions and be aware
of repeating patterns, though, as retrograde Mercury will hover near Venus at
the same time.

During early June business meetings are productive. As the Summer
Solstice nears there is an accent on
community service, politics and charitable endeavors. Honor the longest of
days by preparing a blessing to heal
and uplift those less fortunate. The first
half of July begins quietly; your 12th
house sets the pace, bringing a yen for
rest and reverie. You will cherish the
wisdom and advantages of secrecy.
July 15 through Lammastide expressive Mercury conjuncts your Sun. Your
speaking and writing skills will be in
top form. Others will be persuaded by
your eloquence. You'll greatly enjoy
discussing new ideas at the end of July.
The New Moon in Leo on August 2
forms a grand trine with Uranus and
Saturn, ushering in a four-week cycle
of ease. Expect a breakthrough regarding important goals. Past efforts are
rewarded and appreciated. Adopt a live-and-let-live attitude toward those who
don't agree with you.

September 1 brings an eclipse in
your financial sector. Be receptive to
changes in your source of income. A
demand for a different type of work or
the need to learn a different, salable job
skill could arise before the year ends.
Live within your means and all will be
well. Dedicate the Autumnal Equinox
ritual to a prosperity blessing. Burn
cinnamon incense and wear gold to
encourage extra cash flow during the
season to come.

Prepare for a great deal of coming and going during the first half of
October, as a parade of transits will
activate your 3rd house. A neighbor or sibling can contact you with a
valuable invitation or suggestion. On
October 19 a favorable cycle for love
begins when Venus trines your Sun.
The Halloween season brings happy
times with those you care deeply for.
The King or Queen of Hearts, Cupid or
a favorite childhood character, such as

Little Bo-Peep, would be favorable costume ideas. The good times roll on through November 11.

From late November until December 19 Mars will oppose your Sun. Associates will be quite assertive, even argumentative. Keep the competitive situations good-natured. Let others make decisions and learn through experience. You might have the last laugh in the end. Dedicate the Winter Solstice to a blessing for peace and harmony. Include pine cones on your altar; they will trap any negative energies which might linger.

January brings a mystical Venus-Neptune connection. Friendly spirits or angels are in evidence. Call upon the hidden realms for insight concerning both security issues and spirituality. This is also an excellent month to make a New Year's resolution regarding your health. Plan a wholesome exercise and diet schedule. On January 29 a favorable Mars trend begins and remains through the winter. Your vitality and energy level increase. Much will be accomplished. The Full Moon eclipse in Leo on February 10 highlights your self confidence and effervescence. Opportunities and good fortune increase; growth is the keynote. During March, Venus will turn retrograde in your 9th house. Friendships with foreign-born people or those of a different generation can be enjoyed. Travel plans for the future are finalized as winter draws to a close.

HEALTH

Your cell salt is magnesium phosphate, $Mg_3(PO_4)_2$. It is said to relieve migraine headaches, convulsions, muscle spasms and exhaustion. This cell salt is called "the natural painkiller." It has a healing effect on motor skills and sensory nerves, as well as benefiting the body parts ruled by Leo: the heart, lungs and back. Magnesium phosphate is found in mint, soybeans, plums, wild rice, cashews and citrus fruits.

LOVE

Serious Saturn remains in your love sector all year. A desire for stability, support and commitment prevails. The eclipse in Aquarius on August 18 brings a turning point regarding a close partnership. Be receptive to growth. July and early November promise romantic bliss.

SPIRITUALITY

Your search for spiritual truth is very strong throughout the year to come due to the prominence of transits in your 9th house. You might explore new philosophical concepts. The Full Moon on October 16 and the last weeks of winter will be especially significant regarding spiritual realizations.

FINANCE

From the Vernal Equinox through May 10 Jupiter is retrograde in Virgo, your financial sector. This favors settling old debts and meeting other monetary obligations. May 11 – September 9 Jupiter moves rapidly through Virgo in a favorable aspect to Pluto, promising extra income. The spring and summer favor saving and planning for your long-term financial future.

VIRGO

August 23 – September 22

Spring 2016 – Spring 2017 for those
born under the sign of the Virgin

A retentive memory and a remarkable
concept of detail characterize the intellectual and perceptive Virgo. Ingenious,
versatile and discriminating, you are
the zodiac's perfectionist. Hypercriti-
cal and fastidious, you expect much of
those close to you. You have a skep-
tical side. Your own health and the
well-being of others is frequently an
important focus in your life.

The Vernal Equinox finds you
embroiled in debate and controversy
because Mercury is involved in a tense
mutable aspect pattern. Since elusive
Neptune comes into play, all is not as it
seems. Be patient and observant. Apply
the axiom "least said, soonest mended."
From mid-April through June 12 several favorable Taurus transits, including
Venus and the Sun, will affect your 9th
house. Travel, educational opportunities
and new philosophical perspectives will
brighten your days. May Day favors
designing a flower or vegetable garden.
Gather some vintage ribbons to decorate a Maypole. Enjoy time outdoors.

The Full Moon on May 21 activates
Mars and Saturn in your sector of residence and family life. An issue which
has been brewing for some time might
have to be faced before the end of June.

This could involve a residential move,
maintenance of the home or the needs
of a relative. At the Summer Solstice
bless and clear your living space.

In July helpful friends arrive. A
sense of camaraderie and support prevails through July 20, bolstered by
supportive transits in your 11th house.
As August begins, Mercury will join
Jupiter in your birth sign. Celebrate
Lammastide by donning new garments
and accessories. It's time to honor and
express your individuality. Through
the end of the month a sense of peace
and understanding prevails. Your innate
ability to analyze situations and find
solutions will carry you forward.

September 1 arrives with the New
Moon in Virgo and a solar eclipse conjunct your Sun. Everything goes hay-
wire. Elements of the unexpected rattle
the status quo. Changes of all kinds
touch your life in many ways nearly
every day all month long. Look to the
future. Just equate change with growth
and all will be well in the end. A second eclipse on September 16 affects
all kinds of established partnerships.
Allow others their freedom and respect
their opinions to assure a happy out-
come for all. At the Autumnal Equinox
prepare a hearty, harvest vegetable soup
and whole grain bread. Enjoy the meal
outdoors while admiring the fall colors.
Release the past.

By October a favorable Mars aspect
brightens your 5th house of pleasure
and romance. This lasts through November 9, giving you renewed energy
and enthusiasm. You'll enjoy sports,
hobbies and creative projects. An
adventure hero, athlete or warrior god

or goddess would be an ideal Halloween costume. From mid-November until December 7 a sweet Venus aspect combines with an intense Pluto transit. Love and admiration come your way. A relationship becomes more significant and supportive. A hobby or craft project can add to your income. Try designing handcrafted items to gift at Yule. You will relish time spent relaxing at home during the last three weeks of December. Resurrect sentimental keepsakes for your Winter Solstice altar and prepare a favorite old time recipe during the longest of nights, December 21-22.

In January a strong 7th house emphasis encourages others to make plans involving you. Cooperate if this feels beneficial, but be cautious if you sense that the direction things are heading isn't quite right. As Candlemas nears, communication will improve. Prepare a ritual observance to facilitate good mental rapport with the important people in your life. The solar eclipse on February 26 is significant regarding obligations to others and commitments. March accents your 8th house. Investments and financial management are a focus. March 12 brings the Full Moon in Virgo. This strengthens undercurrents and nuances in relationships. Consider carefully, then choose the best direction for yourself. Ironically, that will help you to do right by others as winter ends.

HEALTH

Potassium sulfate, K_2SO_4, is Virgo's cell salt. This salt keeps the pores open. It has been used to treat acne and is said to keep the skin smooth. It's also an effective treatment for overly dry or oily hair. Virgo rules the lower digestive tract, stress and nerves in general. This cell salt has been used to address those health issues. Maintaining youthfulness, agility and rejuvenation are aided by potassium sulfate. It is found in avocados, Brazil nuts, dill, peaches, green beans, licorice and fennel.

LOVE

Eclipses on September 16 and February 26 affect your 7th house of relationships. Partnerships are evolving. Be receptive to changes. Put the happiness and well-being of a loved one first and all will be well. In May, August and late November through early December, benevolent Venus transits favor true love.

SPIRITUALITY

Neptune, an important spiritual indicator, forms a prominent opposition aspect all year. The actions of others, whether for good or ill, will mirror your own spiritual perceptions. Invitations you receive to attend metaphysical gatherings and ceremonies can profoundly affect your own spiritual path. Interpret symbolic dreams, especially near the Full Moons in May, September, and December.

FINANCE

Near your birthday Jupiter enters your financial sector where it will remain until mid-2017. There will be chances to get ahead financially. Make the most of these. The autumn and winter months promise an optimum time to nurture earning opportunities.

LIBRA
September 23 – October 23
Spring 2016 – Spring 2017 for those
born under the sign of the Scales

Naturally charming with excellent persuasive skills, Librans seek harmony and balance in all situations. Often you gain entry into the most desirable circles, both in business and society. At the same time, material security and a comfortable quality of life are a focus. Relationships and partnerships are especially important.

The Vernal Equinox promises freshness and new beginnings because the lunar eclipse on March 23 is in Libra. Be receptive to growth and change. This year will be memorable. Don't be surprised by the magnitude of changes brewing. It's a time of turning points. During early April there are opposing viewpoints to consider. There can be a debate or some points of controversy to settle near All Fools Day. By mid-month both Mars and Saturn will be retrograde in your 3rd house. A sibling or neighbor seeks your assistance. April is busy. A series of errands and short trips need attention. The pace is exhilarating and hectic.

May Eve is especially fey. Various friendly faeries, elementals and other spirit visitors hover nearby. You might hear of an interesting local haunting by the month's end. Venus is influential May 25 – June 17. Social contacts made at a school or place of worship are significant. This is also a most auspicious time to travel abroad.

At the Summer Solstice career aspirations will occupy your thoughts. You'll cherish secret ambitions to move forward. Dedicate an altar candle to call upon a favorite prosperity god or goddess. July brings positive experiences within your work environment. A presentation you make draws support and admiration. By Lammastide, Mercury joins Jupiter in your 12th house. Your mood will be introspective throughout the rest of the summer. A dream or deep meditation helps you process and release a poignant memory. August through early September brings needed healing for the mind, body or spirit.

In mid-September benevolent Jupiter begins a year-long transit through Libra. Your birthday reveals new opportunities on the horizon. Your luck is changing for the better. At the New Moon in Libra on September 30 select goals for the long-range future. Write a wish list. October 8 – 24 Mercury races through Libra, tagging Jupiter at the Full Moon on October 16. Much information and many new ideas are directed your way. Opportunities for study, travel or your career are all likely to come about. By Halloween the emphasis shifts to home, family life and security issues. Include faux coins and jewels in your costume design this year. Add jeweled and glittery boots or shoes to finish the look with style.

During November Mars, Venus and Pluto will affect your 4th house. Real estate transactions, interior decorating and family gatherings are a focus. Keepsakes and reunions evoke a sentimental mood near Thanksgiving. A cycle of joy begins with holiday events and invitations as the Winter Solstice nears. The good times roll on through New Year's Day.

In January Mars and Neptune will affect your health sector. A dream or intuitive perception brings insight into fitness factors. Seek ways to ease a stressful daily schedule. A much loved animal companion might require extra exercise and attention.

February accents the opinions of others as Venus joins Uranus in Aries. Both planets oppose your Sun. Listen carefully and honor others' freedom of thought even if you disagree. A long-standing partnership might be ending or a new one beginning. The specifics come to light near Valentine's Day. The last half of February brings a favorable Mercury aspect. Your imagination and creativity are in top form. An original idea can solve a problem or generate additional income. Children have much to share. Young people are sources of inspiration, pride and hope.

March accents a desire for order and organization. Your 6th and 8th houses are emphasized during the final weeks of winter. Discard or donate surplus items. Eliminate clutter, and begin spring cleaning early. Research and analysis are helpful regarding a financial plan March 10 – 20.

HEALTH
Libra's cell salt is sodium phosphate, Na_3PO_4. This cell salt is useful in regulating the body's acid/alkaline balance, tired muscles and gout. Also it is said to favorably affect the lower back and kidney function, which are ruled by Libra. Food sources which include sodium phosphate are peas, coconut, corn, brown rice, dandelion greens and sunflower seeds.

LOVE
Of all the birth signs, the specter of aloneness looms largest for you. The year ahead can mean letting go of an old love for one reason or another. Be receptive to a void; you might be unattached temporarily. Future happiness is to come. The August 18 eclipse activates your love sector, and the specifics can come to light near that time. Romantic bliss and happiness are promising September 1 – 23 and December 8 – January 3.

SPIRITUALITY
Mercury, the guardian of thought and communication, rules your 9th and 12th houses, both of which apply to spiritual truths. Spiritual discussion groups and literature assist in processing spiritual ideas. Experiences you have near the eclipses on September 16 and February 26 enhance spirituality.

FINANCE
In September Jupiter, planet of bounty and financial blessings, will enter Libra for a year-long stay. By your birthday splendid financial opportunities will begin to manifest. Be careful not to overextend though. Live within your means or there could be consequences after Jupiter goes retrograde in February.

SCORPIO

October 24 – November 21

Spring 2016 – Spring 2017 for those
born under the sign of the Scorpion

Self-sufficient, with inherent courage
and determination, Scorpio will usually surmount most obstacles. You are
inventive and gifted with leadership
ability. Possessed of an analytical mind
and quick perception, you use strat-
egy to manifest goals. Indifference is
alien to your nature. Your opinions are
almost always passionately pro or con
regarding everything and everyone.

Prepare a love philter at the Vernal
Equinox. Spring's earliest days are
brightened by romantic promise, as
Venus remains in your love sector until
April 4. Overcoming financial challenges is your priority from mid-April
until May 27. Ignite a money-colored,
bright green candle on April 22, the
night of the Full Moon in Scorpio,
and repeat prosperity affirmations.
This can help you focus on correct-
ing a situation which has been drain-
ing your resources. Late May – June
12, Mercury affects your 7th house of
partnerships. Listen while those you're
closest to reveal heartfelt thoughts and
opinions. A loved one might yearn to
write a book, travel or study something
new. Be supportive.

As the Summer Solstice approaches,
Mars conjoins your Sun in your 1st
house. This is a highly competitive
and energetic pattern, lasting through
August 2. Your motivation is exceptionally high. If you can maintain
perspective and avoid overkill, much
will be accomplished. Select peace,
forgiveness and release as themes for
your Lammastide rites. Include blue
along with seasonal colors on your
altar. Try aromatherapy to restore your
inner peace. The eclipse on August 18
highlights your home and family sector. This shows a new agenda regarding
your residence and family life. It's time
to welcome a fresh start.

Early September introduces progressive ideas and contemporary goals. New
associates project a futuristic mood.
Community service can be rewarding.
At the Autumnal Equinox visualize
your heart's desire. September 24 –
October 18 Venus dances through
Scorpio. The bright, colorful autumn
days welcome love and pleasantries
into your life. The fine arts and social
events are woven into these good times.

Late October – November 9 Mars
joins Pluto in your 3rd house. Short journeys, meetings and many conversations
set a busy pace. Stay well informed;
watch the news. At Halloween a sense
of duality prevails. What about a bi-
colored motley, the two faces of Janus
or the comedy and tragedy masks for
a costume?

Mid-November through mid-Dec-
ember emphasizes your 2nd house
of finances. An extra job opportunity
could boost your income. Careful study
of your budget assists in stretching
your hard-earned money. Avoid being
too generous with others near the Full

Moon on December 13. Offer a needy person encouragement and advice instead of financial assistance. At the Winter Solstice Mars enters your sector of love and leisure, a pleasant transit which lasts through January 28. You'll be able to spend more time with children or a favorite hobby. The longest of nights brings a focus on joy and revelry. Add ivy and balsam to your Solstice altar, honoring the jovial spirit of the season.

On January 4 a favorable Venus trend begins, drawing kindness and empathy your way. Music and color can be powerful sources of inspiration as 2017 begins. You'll encounter creative new ideas from others throughout January. Dedicate Candlemas rites to healing. February accents wellness needs, as several transits create a stir in your 6th house of health. A wholesome diet and moderation hold the secret to feeling well. The eclipse on February 11 accents surprising developments in your career field. Stay in tune with new professional trends; update your skills. Mercury joins the eclipse on February 26 in your love sector. There can be a change of heart brewing. Talk over feelings and expectations to avoid misconceptions. Mid-March through the end of winter brings greater understanding and acceptance of life as it is.

HEALTH
Scorpio's cell salt is calcium sulfate, $CaSO_4$. It has been useful in treating the reproductive system and lower bowels, body parts ruled by Scorpio. The reproductive hormones, ulcers and constipation have also responded well to calcium sulfate. It functions as a good overall cleanser to eliminate toxins and facilitate the healing process. This cell salt can be found in currants, cauliflower, horehound and horseradish.

LOVE
Fate is working overtime to create your soul mate connection this year. There are two important eclipses, one on September 16 and one on February 26, in your 5th house of romance. Elusive and mystical Neptune hovers near both. Yearnings which transcend explanation are unfolding. Deepen a love bond by heeding messages which arrive in your dreams. This might involve taking more initiative.

SPIRITUALITY
The New Moon on July 4 highlights your 9th house of spiritual thought and higher consciousness. Enjoy fireworks and sparklers. The explosion of color and light will exhilarate you, opening higher perceptions. Patriotic ideals and activities evoke spiritual awareness during summer's brightest days.

FINANCE
Patience is essential. All year conservative, serious Saturn shadows your financial sector. Develop an impeccable work ethic. Avoid risky ventures. Eventually financial rewards will arrive. Suppress any resentment concerning monetary matters August 3 – September 27. Focus your energy on seeking solutions instead. There is a challenging Mars transit operating then.

SAGITTARIUS

November 22 – December 21

Spring 2016 – Spring 2017 for those
born under the sign of the Archer

Adaptable and ambitious, Sagittarius targets progressive goals. Often these involve exploring academic and intellectual challenges with a desire to compete and win. You're something of a gambler and jovial adventurer. Independent and outspoken, you learn best from experience. You seldom appreciate or heed advice.

From the Vernal Equinox until May 27 fiery, dynamic Mars conjoins your Sun in Sagittarius. You'll be highly motivated and argumentative. Maintain balance and perspective, then much can be accomplished. The New Moon on April 7 conjoins Venus in your sector of love and pleasure. Romantic prospects, hobbies and creative projects are promising through May Eve. On May 21 the Full Moon in Sagittarius provides an opportunity to display your knowledge and skills. Others will be aware of what you have to offer.

June accents your 7th house of partnerships. You'll find it is a time to review your many types of relationships. At the Summer Solstice release a relationship you've outgrown. In regard to business as well as romance, seek progressive associates who bring fresh outlooks.

July begins with several transits activating your 8th house of subtleties. You'll cherish peace and privacy. Research work or solving a mystery can captivate you. Venus enters Leo, your sister fire sign, during mid-July. This eases your workload. Late July favors vacation travel and enjoyment of foreign cuisine or imported items. At Lammas place a globe on your altar to symbolically widen your world. Keepsakes and souvenirs acquired during your travels have a unique magic. Incorporate these tokens into ritual observances.

Mid-August through September 8 Jupiter, your ruler, will be trailed by other transits in your 10th house of career. Opportunities for professional advancement can change your life now. The eclipse on September 1 marks an especially dynamic time regarding the tide of fame and fortune. At the Autumnal Equinox, Mars and Uranus will form strong aspects involving your 1st and 5th houses. Your personality impresses others during late September. An avocation can bring recognition.

October 1 – 18 you'll crave peace and privacy. Stroll through a park and enjoy the colorful foliage to heal and rejuvenate. As Halloween nears, Venus enters your birth sign, bringing an upbeat cycle for both love and money which lasts through November 11. For your Halloween costume this year look to a favorite romantic hero or heroine for inspiration – maybe Casanova, Romeo, Cinderella or Juliet.

Mercury races through your birth sign November 13 – December 2. You will speak and move quickly. It's an excellent time to catch up on correspondence, make travel plans or try some serious writing. During December you will become increasingly focused on security issues. Explore new markets for your viable job skills. Rework your budget and seek financial advice. Prepare a prosperity blessing at the Winter Solstice. Consider burning a miniature Yule log of oak or apple wood on your altar. Toss a bit of frankincense and myrrh into the flames and ask the Lord and Lady for financial assistance.

January accents home and heritage, with Venus, Mars and Neptune in your 4th house. Express tolerance regarding a relative who has been difficult. Seek to make your residence more comfortable and functional. At Candlemas Mars will be in your 5th house, emphasizing a creative plan, excelling at a game or sport, or exploring a love interest. From February 6 through March, Jupiter is retrograde in your 11th house. You'll reevaluate goals, friendships and group affiliations. Past experiences reflect future events.

The eclipse on February 26 affects your family dynamics and residence. Redecorating and remodeling ideas can appeal. A relative makes a surprise announcement in early March. Be diplomatic if you have an urge to voice your concerns or disapproval. On March 10 Mars enters your health sector. Maintain personal wellness by releasing stress. Embrace the healing qualities of peace and quiet.

HEALTH
The Sagittarius cell salt is silicon dioxide, SiO_2. The hip and upper leg regions as well as blood sugar and blood pressure levels are linked to your birth sign. This cell salt has been used to relieve maladies related to those areas. It also has been effective in treating hard-to-heal wounds and promoting good vision and teeth, strong bones and hair growth. Try adding it to the diet to encourage thick, glossy hair growth. Good food sources include oats, chicory and pepper.

LOVE
Uranus hovers in your love sector all year, suggesting sudden meetings and partings. Venus and Mars, the planets of romance and passion, will join Uranus in your 5th house of love from early February through winter's end. This celestial combination promises a transcendent and exciting love cycle. Valentine's Day brings a delightful encounter with Cupid's arrow.

SPIRITUALITY
On September 9 Jupiter enters Libra and begins a benevolent, year-long transit through your 11th house. Friendships will offer spiritual insights and inspiration. Study, travel or attending spiritual celebrations and ceremonies can be significant in paving your spiritual path.

FINANCE
Saturn, the planet of responsibility and parameters, is in the midst of a three-year passage through your birth sign. Keep trying. This underscores the virtues of patience. Maintain an impeccable work ethic. Financial rewards will come in the future through a job well done at present.

CAPRICORN
December 22 – January 19
Spring 2016 – Spring 2017 for those
born under the sign of the Goat

Prudent and reliable with a flair for organization, the Goat succeeds at patiently fulfilling obligations. A subtle and wry sense of humor helps you to rise above rough situations. Employing practical foresight, Capricorn plans for the future. Secrecy is a favorite defense mechanism if unkindness or ridicule is encountered.

The early springtime indicates upsets in the professional sphere. The eclipse on March 23 affects your 10th house of career. Be flexible. Accept how new factors come into play, and all will be well. In April, Mercury enters Taurus, your sister earth sign. This stimulates personal creativity and brings respectful support from others. A combination of positive celestial factors helps you to resolve challenging career situations by early June. Near May Eve, Venus enters your 5th house. There is time for recreation and relaxation. Attend an art show, share a picnic lunch in a park or hike to a scenic overlook.

During June and July Mars will highlight your 11th house. Friends include you in their plans. The expectations of others draw you into group activities or a prominent role within an organization. You might assume the role of mediator or overseer. At the Summer Solstice offer blessings and affirmations for peace and justice. The Full Moon in Capricorn on July 19 is strongly influenced by Pluto. It marks a culmination of old situations and paves the way for a renewal or renaissance. A new phase is beginning. At Lammastide focus on forgiveness and say your farewells.

In August Mars joins Saturn in your 12th house, heightening your sensitivity. You will sense the needs of those less fortunate and want to help. Charitable endeavors will attract you. Early September finds Jupiter joining Venus at your midheaven. This puts a positive spin on your status and career situation. You will be highly visible. Others express admiration and see you as a role model. At the Autumnal Equinox burn sage to cleanse your workplace. Dedicate a candle and select a crystal to protect your cherished goals and reputation. September 28 – November 9 Mars will transit Capricorn. This generates tremendous energy and enthusiasm. Excitement builds during the bright autumn days. The Full Moon on October 16 highlights the specifics. For Halloween consider a superhero costume, perhaps Wonder Woman or Superman. A vintage soldier's uniform would also be suitable. How about Revolutionary or Civil War regalia, or a Scottish kilt?

Venus will be in Capricorn from mid-November through December 7. This promises happiness and good times for Thanksgiving and the start of the winter holiday season. Plan a gathering, and select gifts. Others will be thoughtful and generous. Mercury turns retrograde in your 1st house just before the Winter Solstice. Sentiment is strong. On the longest of nights honor memories and ancestors. A reunion might be planned for late December. People from your past can call or visit unexpectedly. Hum *Auld Lang Syne* and reminisce about the good times, but remember that a leopard doesn't change its spots. The New Moon in Capricorn on December 29 finds you rather weary of dwelling on days gone by. Write a list of wishes and resolutions you'd like to manifest during the year ahead and look toward the future.

Transportation will be a focus during January. Transits in your 3rd house indicate that you might look for a new vehicle or consider alternative travel and transportation arrangements. Mobility issues should be resolved satisfactorily by Candlemas. Dedicate a candle altar to journeys and conveyances. The eclipse on February 11 affects your 8th house. Awareness of other dimensions and the presence of kindly spirit visitors is heightened. Hesitate if an acquaintance suggests a risky investment scheme or business proposal in late February. If something just doesn't feel right to you, back off.

March emphasizes your sector of home and family life. The focus turns toward the welfare and happiness of relatives, including your extended family. A redecorating or remodeling project or even a new residence might be appealing.

HEALTH
The Capricorn cell salt is calcium phosphate $Ca_3(PO_4)_2$. Capricorn rules the knees and the skeletal structure. Try calcium phosphate to strengthen bones and improve dental health. It has also proven effective in treating cases of rheumatism, arthritis and the proper clotting of blood. Calcium phosphate can be found in peanuts, almonds, pistachios, wintergreen and comfrey.

LOVE
This year the springtime is your season of love. A grand trine in the earth signs which is in effect April 6 – June 12 brightens your 5th house of romance. Decorate a love nest with fragrant flowers and herbs to set the mood for blissful interludes. The New Moon on May 6 favors intimacy. The Full Moon on November 14 illuminates the future of an important relationship.

SPIRITUALITY
Jupiter will occupy your 9th house from early spring until September 9. This indicates an awakening of spirituality. Meditation, the study of spiritual texts and visits to sacred sites would help to augment your personal spiritual journey. Observe the high holidays of the spring and summer (Vernal Equinox, Summer Solstice and Lammas).

FINANCE
The lunar eclipse on August 18 falls in your 2nd house of finances. This has a profound impact on the status quo regarding money all year. Expect a change in your source of income. The financial outlook is promising July 13 – August 5 and again December 8 – January 3.

AQUARIUS

January 20 – February 18

Spring 2016 – Spring 2017 for those born under the sign of the Water Bearer

Diplomatic and ever-popular, Aquarians are willing to help and befriend nearly everyone. Original, observant and curious, you relish activities which transcend the tried and true. You can be reserved, guarding your privacy from those who would intrude upon your personal boundaries.

Finances are at the forefront when springtime begins, as your 2nd house is emphasized. A dream or intuitive hunch helps you to resolve monetary concerns. By mid-April activities revolve around family life. A visitor might offer to help with chores or household repairs near May Eve. May 1 – 24 a Venus aspect generates insecurity or mood swings in a loved one. Offer words of encouragement. Be a good listener.

June finds retrograde Mars impacting career matters. Applaud healthy competition. June 13 – 29 a Mercury transit encourages vacation travel. At the Summer Solstice meditate on what happiness and satisfaction mean to you. Early July accents your health sector. The healing qualities of aromas and colors as well as other alternative therapies can do much to optimize wellness of the mind and body. The New Moon on July 4 favors making new resolutions regarding diet and exercise.

The last two weeks of July accent teamwork. Transits in your 7th house emphasize the need to compromise. Be receptive to alternative plans and viewpoints. Dedicate Lammas rites to welcoming serendipity. The eclipse in Aquarius on August 18 affects your entire month. Changes are in the air. Surprising twists and turns will guide you into new situations. Consider your personal wishes and needs apart from the preferences of loved ones.

September finds Mars impacting your 11th house. After weeks of soul searching, you will come to realizations concerning your wishes and goals. Friends are concerned and want to help. Romantic attachments deepen into true love at the Autumnal Equinox when Venus is prominent. Offer a gift of seasonal fruits or flowers to the one who is dearest to your heart. October 1 – 18 highlights your sector of fame and fortune. You will yearn for success and greater recognition. Extensive study, career-related travel or brainstorming sessions with respected associates can all be significant factors in helping you to move forward. By Halloween you'll be feeling more introspective. Mars will be in your 12th house. Quiet appreciation of the night sky and the deeper spiritual significance of the holiday appeals to you. Costume suggestions are a hermit, mad scientist or ghost.

On November 9 Mars enters Aquarius. Your energy level will skyrocket. This accelerated inner fire continues until December 19. Decorating for the holidays, winter sports or gathering unneeded items to donate are activities you might especially enjoy. At the Winter Solstice retrograde Mercury joins the Sun and Pluto in your 12th house. Old and poignant memories surface. Past life regression might be useful to aid in understanding and accepting the present situation. A deep rapport with wild creatures and the spirit of wilderness areas prevails as December ends. It might be enjoyable to decorate a tree with popcorn chains and other treats for the birds and squirrels or stroll outdoors at sunset.

Security issues arise as January begins. Mars and Venus will impact your 2nd house of resources, earnings and cash flow. Enjoy what you have; live within your means. Bargains can be found January 1 – 9. The Full Moon on January 12 highlights your 6th house, accenting connections to animal companions. A new pet might adopt you. The New Moon in Aquarius on January 27 reveals personal interests and projects. A sense of who you are and what your life means is heightened.

At Candlemas loved ones are thoughtful. February is busy with a strong 3rd house which means multitasking. Time passes quickly. Verify your schedule so you arrive in the right places at the right times. The eclipse on February 11 profoundly affects established partnerships and commitments. Expect a shift in the status quo, possibly including a surprise announcement. Late February and early March accent financial considerations. From March 10 through the end of the winter Mars transits your 4th house. This inspires an urge to promote domestic harmony.

HEALTH

Ordinary table salt, NaCl, is the Aquarius cell salt. Usually there is ample sodium chloride in the average diet. Aquarius rules the ankles as well as the circulatory system. Salt intake can affect blood pressure; it impacts fluid tension in the body. A lack of salt might develop following a persistent cold. Table salt can effectively treat a dry mouth or squelch dangerous reactions to venomous insect bites. Good food sources include figs, beets, mangos, seaweed and water chestnuts.

LOVE

May 25 – June 17 Venus enters your love sector, promising romantic bliss. The New Moon on June 4 is a perfect time to declare your intentions and consider a commitment. September favors travel with the one you cherish. December brings you love and appreciation.

SPIRITUALITY

The eclipse on March 23 affects your sector of spirituality. Changes in your spiritual quest begin with the springtime. Breathing exercises such as yoga pranayama or merely breathing fresh air while walking or sitting outdoors can encourage spiritual awakening.

FINANCE

Eclipses on September 1 and 16 and February 26 all affect your finances. Finances can take a roller coaster ride this year. Changes in values, your source of income and financial needs are all likely. Be patient. In the long run you'll do well.

PISCES
February 19 – March 20
Spring 2016 – Spring 2017 for those
born under the sign of the Fish

Intuitive, compassionate and congenial, Pisceans have a special ability to relieve the suffering and anxieties of others. You adore beauty and appreciate artistry, especially dance. Naturally sensitive, you're often quite psychic. Valuable guidance can be gleaned from interpreting your dreams.

Love connections are tinted with tenderness from the Vernal Equinox through April 5 because Venus joins Neptune in Pisces. Nurture a promising relationship. From mid-April through May, your 2nd and 10th houses are strong, making finances and career challenges the focus. Motivation increases, and you'll be quite competitive. Since Mars and Saturn are involved, your professional responsibilities seem challenging. Your workload lightens and pressures ease after May 27.

Time spent at home is especially enjoyable June 1 – 21, as your family sector is brightened by the Sun and Mercury. A household gathering is peppered with lively discussions. Ideas and stories relatives exchange near the New Moon on June 4 will inspire you. A grand trine in water signs forms with the Sun in Cancer, Mars in Scorpio, and Neptune in Pisces from late June

through July 22. The warm summer days promise ease and satisfaction.

At Lammas, Mercury begins a long passage in your sector of partnerships. This lasts until October 7. Others will communicate needs and make suggestions. Listen carefully. You will hear what you need to know concerning an important relationship. New ideas and eclectic interests impress a partner. The eclipses on September 1 and 16 are significant concerning the future path of close relationships and teamwork of all kinds. Permit others to grow.

At the Autumnal Equinox the Sun joins Jupiter in your 8th house, a trend which remains in force throughout October. Investments, an inheritance and other financial matters are a focus. Investigate and gather information. Awareness of past life recollections and the presence of friendly ghosts and spirit guides is heightened during October. A séance or Ouija board session can yield amazing results. Consider a Halloween costume honoring an elemental such as a brownie, troll, mermaid, gnome, elf, etc.

Social contacts and creative ideas boost your career during early November as Venus transits your 10th house. Important responsibilities need attention November 12 – December 2, when both Mercury and Saturn will square your Sun. Maintain a positive mental outlook. Use diplomacy in all that you say or write. Efforts made at this time will bring professional advancement in the future. The first three weeks of December accent awareness of those in need as your 12th house is highlighted. An organization dedicated to community service enlists your help. Keep a perspective, though, and don't be overly generous if it means undue personal sacrifice. By the Winter Solstice, Mercury will be retrograde in your 11th house. Consider your goals and group affiliations. Analyze repeating patterns; they foretell the future. A sense of déjà vu prevails. Examine old photos by the light of your solstice candles to help you make wise choices.

December 20 – January 28 generates enthusiasm and motivation. Mars will transit Pisces. Control anger and impatience though. It's especially important to be constructive in your focus. Venus joins Mars in your 1st house after January 4. Both love prospects and finances are very promising through Candlemas. Honor the holiday by combining a water feature, such as a shell, shark tooth or small fountain, with altar candles. Early February is a quiet time. Extra hours of sleep or meditation can be very healing during the weeks preceding your birthday. The eclipse on February 18 in your 6th house emphasizes the need for good health habits.

The Pisces eclipse on February 26 is pivotal and transformational. A new direction emerges. A strong Mercury influence March 1 – 13 offers a barrage of new insights and information. Travel, current events and studies can all be significant factors. Winter culminates with an accent on finances. Pursue promising potentials for generating extra income.

HEALTH

The cell salt for Pisces is iron phosphate, $Fe_3 PO_4$. This powerful immune system enhancer helps form and maintain the health of red blood cells. Pisces rules the feet, and this cell salt boosts overall strength and steadiness while assisting with the distribution of oxygen throughout the body tissues. Add iron phosphate to your diet by eating apricots, pumpkin, raisins, molasses, yeast, sauerkraut and chamomile.

LOVE

Jupiter blesses your 7th house of partnerships from early spring through the beginning of September. A desirable relationship grows. Partners make suggestions and plans involving you. The eclipse on September 1 is revealing regarding a commitment.

SPIRITUALITY

Pluto rules your 9th house of higher consciousness. While Pluto is retrograde April 18 – September 26, you will reflect upon and integrate spiritual practices. Time spent near the water facilitates awakening spirituality. How about scuba diving in the ocean, visiting a large aquarium or listening to recordings of waterfalls and waves?

FINANCE

Double-check suggestions others make regarding finances during the spring and summer. A Jupiter opposition could allow the actions taken by another to drain your resources. Trust your own judgment, particularly if something sounds too good to be true. From December through January several planetary transits favor monetary gain.

Sites of Awe

Macau

I BEGAN THIS TREK from Hong Kong, a metropolis like no other in the world. Monstrous skyscrapers crowd this island city located in the South China Sea. Hong Kong is one of the busiest of the world class seaports, a hub for Asian products to be shipped to the west.

I have been advised by the concierge at the hotel to be sure not to miss the ruins of an old church, Cathedral of St. Paul, located on the top of the hill near the center of the old city of Macau. I've decided to take his advice. It takes a little time to figure out how to get there. Apparently, I need to take a taxi down to the water; then a ferry to the new city; and a bus from the newly developed city to the old historic part of the city. The church should be easy to find from there.

Once the ferry docks, I walk down the ramp to the bus ready to take me to my hotel. Hotels like The Sands, The Venetian, The Hard Rock Hotel and others dominate this part of the island. I'm on my way to The Hard Rock, located in "The City of Dreams," a grouping of hotels, restaurants, and shops all located under one roof. Time to have dinner and rest up for tomorrow's adventure. It seems like I've left one busy city only to find myself in another. I'm looking forward to tomorrow's slower pace.

Old Macao

It's morning and it's hot! As I leave my hotel and board the bus for the old city, I look back to see all of the glamor and glitz of the surrounding areas — fashion models, limos, tuxedos, door men, glass, crystals and gold everywhere. This hotel and all of the area around it is part of a modern day fantasy world.

It is a very bumpy ride, but as our bus pulls into a lot in the old part of the city, I am once again grateful to be away from the hustle and bustle of the popular part of Macau and thankful to be here. Walking through the old part of Macau, once a Portuguese colony, I see streets filled with quaint shops. Reflected all around me is a combination of Southeast Asia and old world Europe. There are still people selling souvenirs, but there are also many shops that cater to the local people, like food, fabric, clothing, gifts and restaurants, so that the souvenirs and the tourists don't seem to bother me.

Stone staircase

Signs can be found in Portuguese and in Chinese. Being a little familiar with some Mediterranean languages, I can make my way around with very little help. After less than an hour of walking, I find myself at the foot of a set of stone steps, leading to the church façade on the top of the hill.

I'm very excited. The original church was built in about 1600 and the entire back of the church is missing, leaving just the front wall standing and in excellent shape too. There are numerous people climbing the stairs, taking pictures and looking at the fine gardens to the side of the staircase.

The Crypt

Reaching the top of the stairs, I am very impressed to see the condition of the façade. As I take some pictures, I notice a sign to my left that explains the history of the church. Fascinating to see the remains of a church from 400 years ago in a land where you would never expect to see a Christian place of worship. I spend a considerable

amount of time here, taking in the view of the façade from front and back, and then going down to the crypt beneath the ruins. It must be 20 degrees cooler down here — well-lit stone walls, and burial chambers that command silence and respect. I can hear a tour guide instructing his group to be quiet as they enter the crypt.

I'm now coming out of the crypt back into the incredible heat. While looking for a bit of shade, I circle around to the northwest side of the ruin and, behind a wall, I see a very small building that captures my attention. It is a temple, built right next to the church. Not visible from the steps or from the crypt or façade itself, this beautiful old temple is barely big enough for two to four people to step within. Outside are incense burners for offerings and for the temple custodian to keep burning.

Shrine of Na Tcha

I slowly walk to the front door, not sure if it is okay for me to step inside or not. Then, with great care, I step over the ghost threshold (a wooden beam meant to keep ghosts out of the sacred temples). The air is thick with incense and the smell of flowers. There is an elderly woman sitting to the side in a chair. Her hands are folded and her straight black hair covers her eyes. I fold my hands in prayer and bow my head toward her. She just barely nods to acknowledge my presence. Turning to the altar before me and having read the sign outside, I know that this is the Temple of Na Tcha, who is worshiped as a god of protection.

For many years, I have carried an amulet, made from the clay of a sacred river in India. I take this amulet out of my pocket. Placing it on the altar in front of me, I bow in prayer. Prayers for protection — protection of myself, my spouse, my pets, my family, and all the loved ones in my life. As is typical of Asian traditions, I also pray for all beings under the canopy of heaven. May suffering be removed from all of their hearts, and may they be protected from temptation, disease and ignorance. May they not be bound to the trappings of this world.

Ruins and shadows

I take the amulet off the altar, kiss it, and return it to my pocket. I leave some coins and paper in an offering bowl by the side of the altar and bow my head to the old woman as I leave. She says *xiexie* ("thank you" in Chinese).

I leave the temple with my heart feeling lighter. Expecting to be impressed with the magnitude of the ruins of a stone Christian church from 1600, I also left humbled by the small wooden hut in its shadow.

— ARMAND TABER

Reviews

The Sorcerer's Secrets: Strategies in Practical Magick
ISBN-13: 978-1601630599
New Page Books
$12.48

JASON MILLER is by no means a new author in the world of magick and esoterica; he is, however, one that is proving to be a titan amongst a crowd of adequate writers. Miller is unlike many modern magicians. He does not treat the aspiring magician to endless chapters of armchair pondering, rather his approach is practical and filled with the grit of action. In *The Sorcerer's Secrets: Strategies in Practical Magick* Miller has given us an approach to magick that is holistic, hands-on and most importantly achievement oriented.

Miller begins this journey into practical magic with some "basic training" techniques. If this particular tome were only the first four chapters, it would be well worth the investment of time and money. He spends the briefest of chapters providing an overview of magickal theory reviewing his "Three Levels" of magick. This is really all the straightforward theory that will be presented. The remainder of his basic training is devoted to exercises of breathing (where he spends a goodly amount of time) and regular daily practices such as mediation, invocation and energy balancing exercises. Miller's illuminating brief dealing with meditation is brilliant, being deceptively simple but impactful when understood on all levels as a core practice.

The remainder of the book is devoted to practical applications of magick and is very much an "out-of-the-box" treatise. This is not to say that it is a simple spell book. Quite the opposite, Miller's depth of knowledge is evident vis-à-vis the method in which he peppers working with thoughtful reasoning behind practical actions.

Miller has extended *The Sorcerer's Secrets: Strategies in Practical Magick* through his Strategic Sorcery correspondence course, but that is another review. This reviewer will leave you with advice that this is one of those rare books whose power and depth makes it a nightstand book, as well as one you will want to carry with you every day on your e-reader.

Ghosts & Spirits Tarot
ISBN-13: 978-1572816619
U.S. Games Systems Inc.
$18.00

THERE ARE A MYRIAD of theme Tarot decks available. Often an encounter with such decks is fraught with forced imagery and a stretch in metaphors. This is not the case with Lisa

Hunt's *Ghosts & Spirits* Tarot. While you will not find the standard variation of the Rider-Waite imagery, after a close examination of each card and a quick read through of the accompanying booklet, you will realize that this deck's imagery rather than being forced is a visual reinterpretation drawing on ghostly images from the legend and lore of various cultures.

Lisa Hunt's deck is standard in one aspect; it follows a traditional structure of 78 cards, with 22 Major Arcana and 56 Minor Arcana Cards. In the Major Arcana Strength is card VIII and Justice is XI, renaming card V the High Priest (traditionally the Hierophant) and card XIV Chains (traditionally the Devil). She also provides us with alternate names for each Major Arcana card, for example alternately naming the Empress as Guardian Spirt, hinting at the meaning and imagery of the card. In the Minor Arcana, she provides us with the typical suites of Wands, Swords, Cups and Pentacles, and conventionally naming the court cards of each suit King, Queen, Knight and Page.

Hunt provides an additional 79th card, which when it falls in a spread indicates that the reading bears closer examination and reflection. This cards, as is the case with the other cards, is rich in symbol with many faces looking back at you almost as if to say, look at this reading with many sets of eyes from many angles.

The booklet included with the deck provides insightful divinatory meanings which if they were presented by themselves would be well worth in-depth study. This is especially true of the insight provided for the Major Arcana. A prime example would be the meaning presented for the Fool, "…Preserve a child-like optimism as you explore new paths, but bear in mind that anything can happen along the way." This kind of nuance is rarely provided in other quick meanings found in booklets that accompany various decks.

The sepia and muted colors of each card immediately draws you in and you get lost in the beauty of the presentation before you realize that you are surrounded by fantastical images filled with spirits that will speak to you if you allow them but a chance. Each of the cards is thoughtful in its approach to imagery, and only in the rare instance did this reviewer find an image too jarring to make the connection to the divinatory meaning.

The *Ghosts & Spirits Tarot* is indeed a rare find in themed tarot and well worth exploration by those who would like imagery that is off the beaten path of the Rider-Waite deck.

Damh The Bard – Sabbat
Label: Caer Bryn Music
Copyright: 2015 Damh the Bard
Total Length: 49:54
£12.00

DAMH THE BARD'S seventh album *Sabbat* is familiar territory for Witches, Pagans and Druids. It is a fine addition to his catalog, and if you are a dedicated follower of our Almanac you may recall that we have reviewed and recommended Damh's work in previous editions. Along with some new original tunes, he also covers the traditional English ballad "Scarborough

Fair" which was introduced to us by Simon & Garfunkel in their 1966 album *Parsley, Sage, Rosemary and Thyme*, and which was released as a single after being featured on the soundtrack to *The Graduate* in 1968. *Sabbat* also includes a faithful cover of the Uriah Heap song "Lady in Black" from their 1971 album *Salisbury*.

Dahm is one of the trio of people who help to lead the Order of Bards Ovates & Druids and truly lives up to his performing name of "Damh the Druid." Even though we have only included a few of his seven albums, every one of them deserves an honored place in your music collection and on your playlists.

Check out a short video of Damh talking about this effort on the website of Phillip Carr-Gomm, the current leader of the Order of Bards Ovates & Druids – http://www.philipcarr-gomm.com/sabbat-by-damh-the-bard/

You can order the CD online, which also includes unlimited streaming of Sabbat via the free Bandcamp app, plus high-quality download in MP3, FLAC and more. http://store.paganmusic.co.uk/album/sabbat-2

Suns Of Arqa – All Is Not Lost,
But Where Is It ?
Label: Liquid Sound Design
Copyright: 2015 Liquid Sound Design
Total Length: 58:12
£9.00

TRIPPY 21ST CENTURY beats mated with 20th century psychedelia and layered throughout with ancient wisdom tradition flavor. What's not to love about that? This is a collaboration of poetry, music and spirit featuring the extraordinary talents of Raja Ram from "Shpongle," and both Alex Patterson and Youth from "The Orb."

Suns of Arqa are a World Music collective founded in 1979 by Michael Wadada. Since the group's formation, over 200 people from around the world have played and recorded with them, and in many cases these were like-minded musicians Wadada met as he travelled the world. Pioneers of World Beat, Ambient, Downtempo and Electro-Dub, Suns of Arqa draw inspiration from around the world, interpreting indigenous, tribal and classical folk traditions.

They have created an impressive legacy and earned worldwide recognition. Having purchased and appraised the vast bulk of their discography, this reviewer has with great interest followed the Suns Of Arqa and their growth for over 25 years. Their music is unlikely to disappoint and each new offering raises the bar which will require any enthusiast to listen to new purchases with keen ear and a refined palette. This new album surpasses everything that this reviewer has heard from this ensemble. However, that is no reason for the new devotee who enjoys this new album not to take the journey into their back catalog. There is a strong likelihood that you will be set upon a journey of discovery that will take you to new and old worlds of enjoyment.

News from The Witches' Almanac

Glad tidings from the staff

Trolls and Witches

Once again, our warehouse has moved. We have consolidated books from more than one location to a central site. Now we are located in the same building as The Troll Shop and The Witches' Almanac Shop. Please come visit us at 88 Main Sreet, East Greenwich, RI.

Parting Brings Such Sweet Sorrow

After being an editor for *The Witches' Almanac* for a number of years, Judika Illes will be leaving us. She has taken a position with our good friends at Red Wheel/Weiser/Conari – publishers and distributors of metaphysical books located in Newburyport, MA. We would like to thank Judika for all of her hard work and expertise through the years, and we wish her all the very best at her new home.

It's All Social

The Witches' Almanac welcomes Susan Asselin to our staff. Our growing presence on social networks such as Facebook has meant that we were in need of a person with knowledge of both the magical world and the ephemeral cyber world. Susan brings a wealth of occult knowledge, down-to-earth sensibility and social network-ing savvy to bear as moderator of our Facebook page. Drop by and visit with Susan at https://www.facebook.com/thewitchesalmanac, and if you ever make your way to Providence be sure to stop in Susan's shop, Mother Mystic Spiritual Apothecary at 179 Dean St, Providence, RI 02903.

So You Want a Primer

David Conway's *Magic: An Occult Primer* is a seminal work that brought magical training to the every-magician in the early 70s. *The Witches' Almanac* is proud to announce the republishing of this very important work ($24.95 ISBN 978-1-881098-36-2). David is an articulate writer presenting the mysteries in a very workable manner  for the serious student. Along with the updated texts on philosophy and practical magic will be a plethora of graphics that have all been redrawn, promising to be another collector's edition published by *The Witches' Almanac*.

Whoops!

Four essays in the previous edition of *The Witches' Almanac: Fire, the Transformer,* were improperly attributed. They were entitled 'Planetary Hours,' 'The Lesser Banishing Ritual of the Pentagram,' 'Platonic Influence,' and 'Tarot Birthday Correspondences.' These articles were written by Anthony Teth.

Newsworthy

OVER THE YEARS, Raven Grimassi (along with his wife Stephanie) has shared his views and his own brand of Witchcraft with the Pagan community through his many books. Through his prolific writing, he has educated and enriched the spiritual life of many. To date, Raven's writing have focused on practical and hands on methods for both novice and advanced practitioner.

At *The Witches' Almanac*, we have had a chance to discuss a very new and exciting endeavor that the Grimassis have just begun to embark upon. While writing is their native medium, they are equally comfortable in the speaking arena. They  have presented workshops around the country for quite some time. Now, they have begun the next logical step. Raven and Stephanie are now in the production stage of creating a two-hour DVD documentary *Ever Ancient, Ever New: Witchcraft by the Hearthside*. This project will explore the roots and ways of Witchcraft throughout the ages down to modern times.

Some of the topics that this dynamic couple will tackle are:
*   History – Facts and Fiction
*   The Place of Myth and Legend in Witchcraft
*   The Ways of the Witch – a Practice, a Religion, or both?
*   Folkloric Witchcraft
*   Peasant Witchcraft
*   Ceremonial Witchcraft
*   The Old Ones – Spirits and Deities in Witchcraft
*   The Meaning and Use of Tools in Witchcraft
*   The Ritual Circle and Ritual Techniques
*   The Art of Witchcraft – Magical Techniques, Witchcraft as Personal Path of Inner Spirit.

EVER ANCIENT, EVER NEW

WITCHCRAFT BY THE HEARTHSIDE

Raven and Stephanie Grimassi
DVD Documentary

Published cover version may vary

We, at *The Witches' Almanac*, are looking forward to reviewing their DVD, and hope that they are successful in its production schedule for this year. As always with their work, we anticipate that this will shape the Pagan landscape for years to come. In the coming months, please check back with us. We will keep you abreast of the progress of this important endeavor, posting updates at TheWitchesAlmanac.com/NewsandLinks.

From a Witch's Mailbox

Who am I?

How does one know if she/he is really a Witch? – Submitted by Lorraine Margueritte Gasrel Black

Witches discover their vocation in a variety of ways. Some are born to the craft. Many seek out teachers to aid their development after experiencing past life remembrances, dreams or psychic experiences. Knowing one is a witch is like knowing one's gender; it's within your soul. Someone who was not raised as a Witch will often experience a type of inner knowing or awakening. You may find yourself intuitively acting in concert with Nature, being drawn to the Moon and the Stars and hearing the voices of trees and flowers. Witches can often be recognized by other Witches.

Help is on the Way

Can one use "magic" to benefit oneself, or more precisely ones "family" which in turn would result in a benefit or betterment of one's life without negative results? – Submitted by G. Raymond Raulerson

When using properly crafted spells to better oneself and/or family, one should not expect negative results unless malefic magic is involved. If you are working to destroy someone else's

happiness in order to advance yours, the spell may have unintended consequences when you least expect them. Magic to better oneself and/or family is probably the most used contrivance in the Witch's toolbox.

Cold as a What?

Is there any truth to the old superstition that witches have a third nipple? – Submitted by Holly Cornwell

There are many old superstitions about witch marks. It is a long held belief that some physical hallmarks of the Witch are: red hair, moles, warts, birthmarks, extra teeth, extra fingers and toes, insensitive patches of skin and the infamous witch's teat. The witch's teat or third nipple was said to be used to suckle imps. Most of these superstitions originate from the mid-1500s, when this physical evidence was used to "identify" witches and convict those accused of practicing witchcraft.

To Circle or Not

Is it necessary to be within a magic circle for a witch's spell work to be effective? – Submitted by Peter Abruzzi

Casting spells within a traditionally cast magic circle, with or without a coven, is an optimal way to practice magic. However, many times magical work is done in places where this is not possible. The effectiveness of any spell is dependent on the practitioner's knowledge, intention and skill level.

Which Witch is Which

With so many different types of Wicca out there, how do I begin to decide which one is "the way" for me? – Submitted by Courtney S. Alvarez

Hopefully you will have done some research into the beliefs and practices of each tradition before searching for a teacher. Most traditions will make public general ideas of what is expected of their students, so you should know if there is something you are uncomfortable with up-front. Look at the history of a tradition, for the path to Wisdom is old.

Meet and socialize with members of different traditions to get a sense of how they treat one another and see if you feel any connection to them. To commit to a tradition of Wicca is to form a spiritual bond with its members.

Hiding from Mercury

Why does everyone dread when Mercury is retrograde? – Submitted by Dierdre Finley

Mercury retrograde rankles nonbelievers and believers alike while being one of the most misunderstood planetary aspects. Mercury is not actually going backward but appears paused in its orbit waiting for the Earth to catch up to it. While Mercury takes a rest as such, everything he rules is left to its own. Most people depend on some type of technology for their daily tasks, so when Mercury is sleeping on the job the support of our tech devices can become

unreliable. During a retrograde period, communication's ruler is taking a nap so people tend to speak without thinking or blurt things out they really didn't want to say. To survive a Mercury retrograde requires one to slow down, expect the unexpected and be prepared to utilize back-up plans. For the unprepared, it can feel catastrophic.

Let us hear from you, too

We love to hear from our readers. Letters should be sent with the writer's name (or just first name or initials), address, daytime phone number and e-mail address, if available. Published material may be edited for clarity or length. All letters and e-mails will become the property of The Witches' Almanac Ltd. *and will not be returned. We regret that due to the volume of correspondence we cannot reply to all communications.*

The Witches' Almanac, Ltd.
P.O. Box 1292
Newport, RI 02840-9998
info@TheWitchesAlmanac.com
www.TheWitchesAlmanac.com

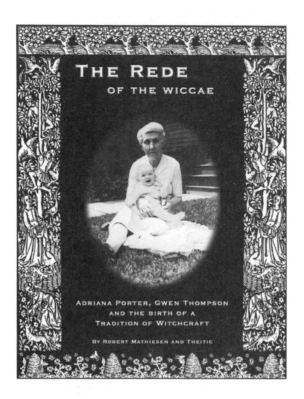

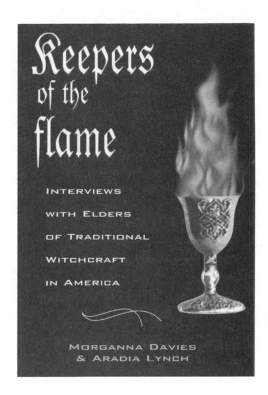

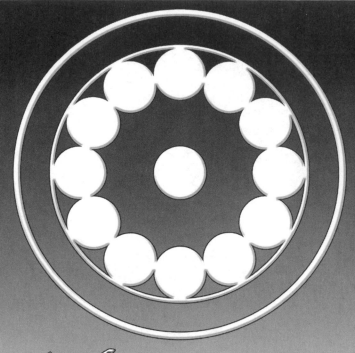

The products and services offered above are paid advertisements.

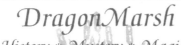

⌒ CLASSIFIED ⌒

TO: The Witches' Almanac
P.O. Box 1292, Newport, RI 02840-9998
www.TheWitchesAlmanac.com

Name_____

Address_____

City_____ State_____ Zip_____

E-mail_____

WITCHCRAFT being by nature one of the secretive arts, it may not be as easy to find us next year. If you'd like to make sure we know where you are, why don't you send us your name and address? You will certainly hear from us.

The Witchcraft of Dame Darrel of York

Charles Godfrey Leland

Introduction by Robert Mathiesen

The Witches' Almanac presents:

- *A previously unpublished work by folklorist Charles Godfrey Leland.*
- *Published in full color facsimile with a text transcript.*
- *Forward by Prof. Robert Mathiesen.*

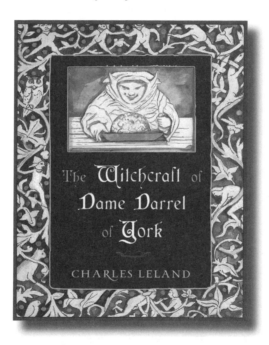

This beautifully reproduced facsimile of the illuminated manuscript will shed light on an ancient tradition as well as provide the basis for a modern practice. It will be treasured by those practicing Pagans, scholars, and all those fascinated by the legend and lore of England.

Standard hardcover edition ($65.00).
Deluxe numbered edition with slipcase ($85.00).
Exclusive full leather bound, numbered and slip cased edition ($145.00).

For further information visit http://TheWitchesAlmanac.com/damedarrel.html

ARADIA
GOSPEL OF THE WITCHES
Charles Godfrey Leland

ARADIA IS THE FIRST work in English in which witchcraft is portrayed as an underground old religion, surviving in secret from ancient pagan times.

• Used as a core text by many modern neo-pagans.

• Foundation material containing traditional witchcraft practices

• This special edition features appreciations by such authors and luminaries as Paul Huson, Raven Grimassi, Judika Illes, Michael Howard, Christopher Penczak, Myth Woodling, Christina Oakley Harrington, Patricia Della-Piana, Jimahl di Fiosa and Donald Weiser. A beautiful and compelling work, this edition has brought the format up to date, while keeping the text unchanged. 172 pages $16.95

❧ *Newly expanded classics!* ❧

The ABC of Magic Charms
Elizabeth Pepper

SINCE THE DAWN of mankind, an obscure instinct in the human spirit has sought protection from mysterious forces beyond mortal control. Human beings sought benefaction in the three realms that share Earth with us — animal, mineral, vegetable. All three, humanity discovered, contain mysterious properties discovered over millennia through occult divination. An enlarged edition of *Magic Charms from A to Z*, compiled by the staff of *The Witches' Almanac*. $12.95

The Little Book of Magical Creatures
Elizabeth Pepper and Barbara Stacy

A loving tribute to the animal kingdom

AN UPDATE of the classic *Magical Creatures*, featuring Animals Tame, Animals Wild, Animals Fabulous – plus an added section of enchanting animal myths from other times, other places. *A must for all animal lovers.* $12.95

♣ a lady shape-shifts into a white doe ♣ two bears soar skyward
♣ Brian Boru rides a wild horse ♣ a wolf growls dire prophecy

A Treasury from past editions...

Perfect for study or casual reading, Witches All *is a collection from* The Witches' Almanac *publications of the past. Arranged by topics, the book, like the popular almanacs, is thought provoking and often spurs me on to a tangent leading to even greater discovery. The information and art in the book – astrological attributes, spells, recipes, history, facts & figures is a great reminder of the history of the Craft, not just in recent years, but in the early days of the Witchcraft Revival in this century: the witch in an historical and cultural perspective.* Ty Bevington, Circle of the Wicker Man, Columbus, Ohio

Absolutely beautiful! I recently ordered Witches All *and I have to say I wasn't disappointed. The artwork and articles are first rate and for a longtime* Witches' Almanac *fan, it is a wonderful addition to my collection.* Witches' Almanac *devotees and newbies alike will love this latest effort. Very worth getting.*

Tarot3, Willits, California

GREEK GODS IN LOVE

Barbara Stacy casts a marvelously original eye on the beloved stories of Greek deities, replete with amorous oddities and escapades. We relish these tales in all their splendor and antic humor, and offer an inspired storyteller's fresh version of the old, old mythical magic.

MAGIC CHARMS FROM A TO Z

A treasury of amulets, talismans, fetishes and other lucky objects compiled by the staff of *The Witches' Almanac*. An invaluable guide for all who respond to the call of mystery and enchantment.

LOVE CHARMS

Love has many forms, many aspects. Ceremonies performed in witchcraft celebrate the joy and the blessings of love. Here is a collection of love charms to use now and ever after.

MAGICAL CREATURES

Mystic tradition grants pride of place to many members of the animal kingdom. Some share our life. Others live wild and free. Still others never lived at all, springing instead from the remarkable power of human imagination.

ANCIENT ROMAN HOLIDAYS

The glory that was Rome awaits you in Barbara Stacy's classic presentation of a festive year in pagan times. Here are the gods and goddesses as the Romans conceived them, accompanied by the annual rites performed in their worship. Scholarly, light-hearted – a rare combination.

CELTIC TREE MAGIC

Robert Graves in *The White Goddess* writes of the significance of trees in the old Celtic lore. *Celtic Tree Magic* is an investigation of the sacred trees in the remarkable Beth-Luis-Nion alphabet; their role in folklore, poetry, and mysticism.

MOON LORE

As both the largest and the brightest object in the night sky, and the only one to appear in phases, the Moon has been a rich source of myth for as long as there have been mythmakers.

MAGIC SPELLS AND INCANTATIONS

Words have magic power. Their sound, spoken or sung, has ever been a part of mystic ritual. From ancient Egypt to the present, those who practice the art of enchantment have drawn inspiration from a treasury of thoughts and themes passed down through the ages.

LOVE FEASTS

Creating meals to share with the one you love can be a sacred ceremony in itself. With the witch in mind, culinary adept Christine Fox offers magical menus and recipes for every month in the year.

RANDOM RECOLLECTIONS II, III, IV

Pages culled from the original (no longer available) issues of *The Witches' Almanac*, published annually throughout the 1970's, are now available in a series of tasteful booklets. A treasure for those who missed us the first time around; keepsakes for those who remember.

ORDER FORM

Each timeless edition of *The Witches' Almanac* is unique.
Limited numbers of previous years' editions are available.

Item	Price	Qty.	Total
2016-2017 The Witches' Almanac – Air	$12.95		
2015-2016 The Witches' Almanac – Fire	$12.95		
2014-2015 The Witches' Almanac – Earth	$12.95		
2013-2014 The Witches' Almanac – Moon	$11.95		
2012-2013 The Witches' Almanac – Sun	$11.95		
2011-2012 The Witches' Almanac – Stones, Powers of Earth	$11.95		
2010-2011 The Witches' Almanac – Animals Great & Small	$11.95		
2009-2010 The Witches' Almanac – Plants & Healing Herbs	$11.95		
2008-2009 The Witches' Almanac – Divination & Prophecy	$10.95		
2007-2008 The Witches' Almanac – Water	$9.95		
2006-2007 The Witches' Almanac – Air	$8.95		
2005-2006 The Witches' Almanac – Fire	$8.95		
2004-2005 The Witches' Almanac – Earth	$8.95		
2003-2004 The Witches' Almanac – Air	$8.95		
2002-2003 The Witches' Almanac	$7.95		
2001-2002 The Witches' Almanac	$7.95		
2000-2001 The Witches' Almanac	$7.95		
1999-2000 The Witches' Almanac	$7.95		
1998-1999 The Witches' Almanac	$6.95		
1997-1998 The Witches' Almanac	$6.95		
1996-1997 The Witches' Almanac	$6.95		
1995-1996 The Witches' Almanac	$6.95		
1994-1995 The Witches' Almanac	$5.95		
1993-1994 The Witches' Almanac	$5.95		
The Witchcraft of Dame Darrel of York, clothbound	$65.00		
Aradia or The Gospel of the Witches	$16.95		
The Horned Shepherd	$16.95		
The ABC of Magic Charms	$12.95		
The Little Book of Magical Creatures	$12.95		
Greek Gods in Love	$15.95		
Witches All	$13.95		
Ancient Roman Holidays	$6.95		
Celtic Tree Magic	$7.95		
Love Charms	$6.95		
Love Feasts	$6.95		
Magic Charms from A to Z	$12.95		
Magical Creatures	$12.95		
Magic Spells and Incantations	$12.95		
Moon Lore	$7.95		
Random Recollections II, III or IV (circle your choices)	$3.95		
SALE 20 back issues with free book bag and free shipping	$100.00		
The Rede of the Wiccae – *Hardcover only*	$49.95		
Keepers of the Flame	$20.95		
Subtotal			
Tax (7% sales tax for RI customers)			
Shipping & Handling (*See shipping rates section*)			
TOTAL			

BRACELETS			
Item	Price	Qty.	Total
Agate, Green	$5.95		
Agate, Moss	$5.95		
Agate, Natural	$5.95		
Agate, Red	$5.95		
Amethyst	$5.95		
Aventurine	$5.95		
Fluorite	$5.95		
Jade, African	$5.95		
Jade, White	$5.95		
Jasper, Picture	$5.95		
Jasper, Red	$5.95		
Lapis Lazuli	$5.95		
Malachite	$5.95		
Moonstone	$5.95		
Obsidian	$5.95		
Onyx, Black	$5.95		
Opal	$5.95		
Quartz Crystal	$5.95		
Quartz, Rose	$5.95		
Rhodonite	$5.95		
Sodalite	$5.95		
Tigereye	$5.95		
Turquoise	$5.95		
Unakite	$5.95		
Subtotal			
Tax (7% for RI customers)			
Shipping & Handling *(See shipping rates section)*			
TOTAL			

MISCELLANY			
Item	Price	Qty.	Total
Pouch	$3.95		
Matches: *10 small individual boxes*	$5.00		
Matches: *1 large box of 50 individual boxes*	$20.00		
Natural/Black Book Bag	$17.95		
Red/Black Book Bag	$17.95		
Hooded Sweatshirt, Blk	$30.00		
Hooded Sweatshirt, Red	$30.00		
L-Sleeve T, Black	$20.00		
L-Sleeve T, Red	$20.00		
S-Sleeve T, Black/W	$15.00		
S-Sleeve T, Black/R	$15.00		
S-Sleeve T, Dk H/R	$15.00		
S-Sleeve T, Dk H/W	$15.00		
S-Sleeve T, Red/B	$15.00		
S-Sleeve T, Ash/R	$15.00		
S-Sleeve T, Purple/W	$15.00		
Postcards – set of 12	$3.00		
Bookmarks – set of 12	$1.00		
Magnets – set of 3	$1.50		
Promo Pack	$7.00		
Subtotal			
Tax (7% sales tax for RI customers)			
Shipping & Handling *(See shipping rates section)*			
TOTAL			

SHIPPING & HANDLING CHARGES

BOOKS: One book, add $5.95. Each additional book add $1.50.

POUCH: One pouch, $3.95. Each additional pouch add $1.50.

MATCHES: Ten individual boxes, add $3.95.
One large box of fifty, add $6.00. Each additional large box add $7.95.

BOOKBAGS: $5.95 per bookbag.

BRACELETS: $3.95 per bracelet.

Send a check or money order payable in U. S. funds or credit card details to:

The Witches' Almanac, Ltd., PO Box 1292, Newport, RI 02840-9998

(401) 847-3388 (phone) • (888) 897-3388 (fax)
Email: info@TheWitchesAlmanac.com • www.TheWitchesAlmanac.com